LOVE-SONGS

Published @ 2017 Trieste Publishing Pty Ltd

ISBN 9780649502462

Love-Songs by George Barlow

Edited by Trieste Publishing Pty Ltd.
Cover @ 2017

www.triestepublishing.com

GEORGE BARLOW

LOVE-SONGS

Trieste

POETICAL WORKS

OF

GEORGE BARLOW.

—————

POEMS AND SONNETS. In Three Parts. 1871.

A LIFE'S LOVE. 1873.

UNDER THE DAWN. 1875.

THE TWO MARRIAGES: a Drama. 1878.

THROUGH DEATH TO LIFE. 1878.

THE MARRIAGE BEFORE DEATH, AND OTHER POEMS. 1878.

TIME'S WHISPERINGS. 1880.

—————

"Mr. Barlow writes not merely fluently but with a command of both language and thought. . . . . His verse is full of promise."—*Westminster Review*.

"Mr. Barlow has not only a fluent pen but an indubitable gift of beautiful and harmonious expression. He is no careless workman, trusting to the force of genius alone and neglecting the strictness of method and the grace of form. Indeed, grace and finish are the conspicuous and prevailing qualities of his poetry." —*Literary World*.

"Mr. Barlow's chief excellence is the way in which he weaves the world of nature external to him with the fancies of imagination and the feelings of the human heart; hence it is that his poetry—which we can cordially commend to all lovers of the muse —is full of similes drawn from the world of external nature."— *Standard*.

LOVE-SONGS.

BY

GEORGE BARLOW,

AUTHOR OF "TIME'S WHISPERINGS," "THROUGH DEATH TO
LIFE," ETC.

"If ' poets are all who love, who think great truths and tell them,
and the truth of truths be *love*,' then Mr. Barlow is a poet of no
mean order."—*British Quarterly Review.*

London:

REMINGTON AND CO.,
133, NEW BOND STREET, W.
[*Removed from 5, Arundel Street, Strand.*]

1880.

CONTENTS.

CONTENTS.

LOVE-SONGS.

———

DAISY'S THIMBLE.

I.

O dear small thimble
Which fingers nimble
Have used so daintily, scores of times,
    I hold you lightly,
    Shining so brightly,
And think of your wearer in far new climes,
    When these same fingers
    O'er which love lingers,
Will turn the pages no more of my rhymes.

II.

These hands, here growing
Like blossoms blowing,
So white and tender, so soft and still,
    Youth's golden flowers
    In life's first hours,
In meadow and coppice, by stream and rill,
    Have gathered : now never
    For ever, for ever,
Our English roses their touch will thrill.

B

III.

Good-bye, good-bye to you,
My verses sigh to you,
O dainty finger that wearest the shell,—
The silver agile
Dear thimble fragile
Whose daily glitter I know so well;
See how I take you
For her sweet sake, you
Small silver token, which unseen fell.

IV.

Fell from her finger,
Fated to linger
Henceforth for ever in secret lair;
Yea, when the owner,
Unconscious donor,
Is breathing the arid and Eastern air,
Thou shalt be sign to me,
Breathe a soft line to me,
Memory of hours and flowers that were.

V.

The fingers that used thee,
Daintily bruised thee
With soft sweet pressure of snow-white tips,
Will no more glitter
Amid the litter,
The spangled litter of work-room snips—
They soon the roses
That Love discloses
Must gather, growing as grow the lips.

VI.

The sacred flowers
Of Love's deep bowers
They soon shall gather, those fingers dear;
    They pass away from us,
    A sun-sweet ray from us,
To lands where suns strike rapid and sheer;
    They leave us, grieve us,
    Sadden, bereave us,
Just at the dawn of the rosebud year.

VII.

O dawning rosebud,
    Whiter than snows bud,
Pass forth and gladden the strange far land;
    Leave our pale bowers
    And storm-swept flowers
Behind, and gather in white quick hand
    The fairy legions
    Of blossoms in regions
Unknown, untrodden, a stranger strand.

VIII.

Thine hands have lingered,
    Plucked and have fingered
English hair-bells, whose stems were slight;
    English roses
    And hedge-side posies
Which laughed, upgazing with laughing might
    Into the fairer
    Eyes, bluer and rarer,
Which pierced the blossoms like star-rays bright.

IX.

These were the flowers
Of tender hours
Of girlhood, laughing as laughed the maid :—
These were the first days,
Free from love's thirst days,
Soft happy moments while love delayed
His ardent coming,
Nor yet the humming
Of his swift wings over the young winds strayed.

X.

This was the May-time
Of growth and of playtime,
The season wherein the plumes were shaped
That, snow-white pinions,
In new dominions,
Snow-white, or lovely and rainbow-draped,
Shall soon remind us
That time did blind us
While one more blossom its sheath escaped.

XI.

A blossom growing
Without our knowing,
To shine, full-petalled, in other fields ;
To gleam, bright-golden,
Not in the olden
Sad land which yearly its tribute yields
To India's younger
Yearning and hunger,
A rose to blazon the flag she wields.

XII.

If ever returning,
The full rose, burning,
Bright, full-grown, beautiful, lights our shore,
What will it say to us,
Soft yea or nay to us ;
Will it be mindful of days before ?
Will it forget them,
Leave or regret them,
Will there be one look soft as of yore?

XIII.

Will there be one look,
Star-look or sun-look,
Sweet as the smiles were, tender of old,
A soft smile starry
For hope to carry
Upward in arms that clasp it and fold
The dear look beaming,
Lightening and gleaming,
In from our chill land's vapour and cold?

XIV.

If ever again to us,
Thrice welcome then to us,
The rose returneth, ah ! shall we know
The same shape older,
The curve of shoulder,
The innocent young lips ? Will there be glow
Of recognition,
O rosebud vision—
Ah, who can tell us ?—time's waves fast flow.

XV.

Yea, faster even
    Than ripples in heaven
Of love's fair ocean, love's moonlit streams;
    Fierce time advances
    With surge-white lances,
Across life's furrows his huge wave gleams;
    His ponderous massive
    Charge, stubborn and passive,
Bears force more cogent than love's frail dreams.

XVI.

So rose returning
    With petals burning
Clear-shaped, love-reddened, across the foam,
    We may not know thee,
    May pass, forego thee;
A foreign blossom not formed at home
    Thou then may'st seem to us,
    A distant dream to us,
No straight stalk fashioned in English loam.

XVII.

So it may be then!
    What shall we see then?
The English Daisy—or some strange stem
    With new grafts clinging
    Not of our bringing,
And our hands having no part in them?
    Nor our hearts knowing
    The weird buds growing,
Whose garish colours our eyes contemn.

XVIII.

O Daisy simple,
With sweet smile-dimple,
Oh, keep thine eyes on thine English name :—
Be ever Daisy
Through Indian hazy
Strange summers when heaven one widelit flame
Burns fierce above thee ;
So shall we love thee
Though ceasing more of thy life to claim.

XIX.

Be English rosebud,
Through fierce sky glows, bud
Above thee, paling thy tender bloom ;
White, white for ever,
In soul changed never,
But deepening only in pure perfume :—
Lifted by passion
In sweet true fashion,
As years flit by thee, and swift consume.

XX.

And thou, small token,
Shapely, unbroken,
I'll keep thee by me till she returns,
In sign that, moulding
To woman, but holding
In safe sweet keeping, Love o'er her yearns ;
I kiss the thimble,
Whose bright shield nimble
From nimble fingers the needle spurns.

TO THE UNIVERSE-GOD.

I.

O God who broodest o'er the ocean spaces,
  And shinest in the gold-winged glimmering cars
Wherein night's steeds are yoked for heaven-high
    races,—
  Splendid amid the cream-white hosts of stars,
Divine and fragrant in all flowery places,
Awful where red-lipped War his pale bride chases,
        Glory his white-lipped bride
          Through battle's foaming tide,—
Great God serene amid the bloodless faces
        Of all the outstretched dead,
        And golden on the head
That shines with girlish golden hair and graces
          Some half-grown rosebud girl,—
          And foam-white in the curl
Of waves that scour the sand with ravenous paces,—
Oh lift the yearning world, swift day by day,
With sweet victorious pulse along its stedfast way!

II.

Thou art in heaven and in the utter deep
  Of fiery flame-winged hell, and in the light
Of suns and moons and in the spotless sleep
  Of children,—in their glances clear and bright:
Thou art in the golden corn the reapers reap,
And in the thundering cataracts that leap
        Along the shaking rocks;
        Thou art in the snow-white flocks

And in the April tender buds that peep
             With laughter through the panes;
             Thou art in the blood-red stains
•Of crime, and in all daring deeds that keep
             Earth's tidal waters pure;
             And through sin's groves obscure
Thou passest as a breeze with wings that weep,—
In all the vales of earth and in the sky
Thy white strange glory, God, we, worshipping,
   descry.

III.

But, most of all, thou shinest in the fair
   Splendour of man and in the tender heart
Of woman, and in love's rose-gladdened air:
   All loveless souls thou piercest with thy dart,
Through passionless pale flesh thine arrows tear,
And cowardly souls thou tanglest in a snare,—
             Thou scourgest them until
             Thou hast thy final will,
Yea, till the fruits of flower-sweet love they bear;
           Thou art within the rose
           Of love when first it glows,
A joy, a deep delight, a wonder rare;
            Thou art within the bloom
            Of passion, a perfume
That brings the utter peace of heaven's hope there;
Thou hast thy crown eternal in the power
Whereby all budding loves burst into burning
   flower.

THE LAST FAREWELL.

Ten years ago the sweet sea shone supreme
With glow and splendour of love's early dream;
Passion touched every wave with magic gleam.

The white waves, laughing, foamed anear our feet;
The summer afternoons, 'mid flowers, were sweet;
We wandered through the woods, the golden
    wheat.

Now where art thou? And, sweetheart, where
    am I?
Where are the sunsets of that early sky?
Love's silver streams have vanished; they are dry.

Thou hast chosen—keep to it—thy fitting part,
And given away thy spirit, and thy heart;
My thought no longer lingers where thou art.

Lo! our great rose of love I take in hand,
And, glancing once back, towards the fair lost
    land,
I let thy face with its sweet breath be fanned.

Once more, once more; then towards a shoreless
    sea,
And mountains where thou mayest not follow me,
I pass; God's world is wide; we both are free.

Or rather free thou art not! thou art bound,
Fettered by this world's anklets to its ground;
Thou hast lost thy wreath; thy chaplets are un-
    wound.

If thou art gone, all roses are not dead;
The fair white lily lifts, for thee, its head;
Thy voice is hushed; the May-winds speak instead.

Still, though not round thy feet, the grasses blow,
The woods, the sea-side hanging woods we know,
Watch the fern-fronds unfasten, row by row.

If thou art dead, the old live waves are white;
The old moon glimmers o'er the old tracks at
    night;
The same sun climbs the flashing midday height.

Thy ghost, thy phantom, fleeteth into air;
And, where it was, this summer rose is fair,
Sweet with the smell still of thy waving hair.

Thou hast not strength to face the fiery morn;
I leave thee; not with anger, not with scorn;
As twilight, when the golden day is born.

Yea, thou art twilight; glimmer with thy face
Once more upon my path, then let the race
Begin for me that leads to love's embrace.

To love's embrace; but, lost love, not to thee;
Unto mine heart "Long-bound heart, thou art
    free,"
I say; "unfettered, chainless as the sea."

Farewell, farewell; along the winds my cry
Sounds, like the sea's wail when the storm is high,
When the pent sea-shriek mixes with the sky.

Farewell, farewell; no kiss, nor grasp of hand;
·Only one look from seaward towards the land;
Thou, blind, art dead; God lives to understand.

May 15, 1879.

A DEATH-SONG.

Bury me not
In some lone spot,
Though tender flowers be there of love's own
training ;
Yea, not the meadow-sweet
And ferns about my feet
Would keep my lonesome spirit from complaining ;
My soul would fly afar
Where human spirits are,
In sight of human forms some solace gaining.

Take me to where
In weighted air
Of mine own well-beloved eternal city
Great fervid thoughts arise,
Yea, where men's glowing eyes
Gleam ever with fresh hope or love or pity ;
Oh set me but within
London's impassioned din,
And even my dead pale lips may chant a ditty.

Plant fragrant bloom
Above my tomb,
Yea, all the season's gentlest maiden flowers ;
Ferns, and the creamy grace
Of lilies thereon place,

And build above me rose-hung shaded bowers;
      But take my body not
      To any country plot,
There to be tortured by the brainless showers.

      Let flowers of thought
      To me be brought,
Yea, all the pent-up city's burning treasures;
      When lovers young begin
      Their new sweet life to win,
Let me in spirit smile amid their pleasures;
      Let the strange sunset red
      That crowns dim London's head
Be the first air of heaven my wing-sweep
  measures.

      Not by the sea
      Oh bury me,
Not 'mid the white waves desperate and foaming;
      Some gentle forest grave
      I would the sooner have
And join the nightjars there amid the gloaming,
      And bloom in meadow-sweet
      And touch the lingering feet
Of lovers through that moonlit forest roaming.

      That would be peace,
      Yet not release .
From all the life-long load of care and craving;
      The life of tender flowers
      And joy of woodland hours

Balm to my spirit cleansing, soft, and saving,
    Doubtless would sometimes give—
    Yet there I should not *live*,
But only sleep, the green leaves round me
  waving.

    No rest I crave,
    No quiet grave,
But ceaseless passionate life,—yea, this for ever;
    A living spirit high
    I would not stoop to die
Or cease the old songful turbulent endeavour;
    I would for ever know
    Sweet love, though that be woe,
And passion, though its pain abateth never.

    Give me, O Death,
    Not slumbering breath
As of a child, but all a man's completeness;
    Grant me the perfect strength
    And risen power at length
Of man, and pour upon me woman's sweetness
    From lips of women dear
    Whom thy hand may bring near,
Staying for me their heavenly swift-foot fleetness.

    Yea, not the tomb,
    But woman's bloom,
Deathless, immortal, perfect, endless, holy—
    Let this, my meadow-sweet,
    My dawning spirit meet,

Trembling with tender footstep, soft and slowly,
  Towards my new-born desire,
  Waking my spirit-lyre
Again, and all mine heart renewing wholly.

  Let such indeed,
  Death, be my meed,
Reward supreme, surpassing, beatific ;
  Deathless am I, O Death,
  If but the pure flower-breath
Of woman in life-giving tides pacific
  Wander above the mould
  Which doth my body hold ;
I fear not then thy dart and lunge terrific.

  I fear thee not
  If but my lot
Bring me love's sacred gifts and spotless favour :
  Yea, if love's utmost glow
  My living soul may know
And love's fruits innermost most precious savour,
  Methinks I have a force
  Thee, pale Death, to unhorse,
And never at thy thundering tilt need waver.

  O woman sweet
  Whose gentle feet
Have brought me in this world mine holiest
 blessing,
  Be near me, kiss me, when
  No help avails of men,

But only thine help, godlike and caressing;
  Lift me above the tomb,
  Yea, sever thou the gloom,
And deaden thou death's fleshly pangs distressing.

  Divide with me
  Death's foaming sea,
Smiling defiance at death's sable minions;
  Cleave thou the sounding air,
  Sweet—open me a fair
Road into heaven by white surge of thy pinions;
  Bid all the stormy waves
  Be still, and grass-grown graves
Be but as love's rose-perfumed pure dominions.

  Rise with me, love,
  This life above,
Long ere the actual death the doorway shadeth;
  That when his real step sounds,
  And his cold breath abounds,
And his deep sword our fast-joined heart invadeth,
  Victors already we
  May, in our calm strength, be—
And conquerors then, as each the other aideth.

  Then in no tomb,
  No death-crowned gloom,
We—you and I, sweet love—will rest or tarry;
  No blossoms shall we need,
  Nor priests to intercede,

C

Nor prayers our air-light souls towards heaven to
    carry :
        For death died long ago
        When, white as just-fallen snow,
God stooped, august from heaven, our souls to
    marry.

EARLY POEMS.

I.

AN EARTH-SONG.

I.

That I could sing the splendour,
And some account could render
Of all the joys of living like a man upon the earth ;
The wonder of the daytime,
The greenery of May-time,
The mystery of death-time, the mystery of birth !

II.

That I could pierce the ether,
The earth—and plunge beneath her
Wide-rolling prairie-panoply of surface-smiles and
flowers ;
And get me to the centre,
And find the fires that rent her
Cliffs and chasms and mountain-tops, the live vol-
canic powers !

III.

Returning to things human,
I'd sing of man and woman,
And all the life of love-time, the glory of the land ;
How man is handed over,
A child become a lover,
From woman unto woman, from tender hand to
hand.

IV.

Man leaves at last his mother,
And findeth in another
A wondrous new development of love that ceaseth
never ;
More wonderful than dreams were,
Fulfilled with fairyland, fair
Fruition of the fancy-realm that seemed a myth
for ever.

V.

And as he sits a-dreaming,
Along his brain is streaming
A river of recollection that linketh old and new ;
He sees the realization
Of childhood's admiration
Of doughty deeds of heroes, of the beautiful and
true.

VI.

How clearly he remembers
By stirring up the embers
Of memory, how Woman first appeared in childish
dreams ;
A goddess of the ether
Who smiled on men beneath her,
All garmented in sunset, and bright with burning
beams.

VII.

Calm, crowned, an earthly centre,
Her robes without a rent, her

Presence an embodiment of all we fancied fair ;
    With eyes of wondrous seeming,
    With tenderness all gleaming,
And a light upon her raiment, and a glory in her
  hair.

VIII.

    One hardly likes to think of it,
    Again in dreams to drink of it,
A draught of joy so wonderful, a picture passing
  pure ;
    And yet, not all ungrateful,
    We are glad that in the hateful
Dark lanes of later life a ray of light can still endure.

IX.

    A memory of the vision,
    The dream, the intuition,
The God-vouchsafed glimpses of the life that
  ought to be ;
    Ah me ! the early river,
    The flakes of light that quiver
Across its course miles upward from the weary
  weary sea !

X.

    It leaps along the sandbanks
    And laughs atween the fern-ranks,
With splashing and with dashing, and with
  sounds of happy glee ;
    It has not seen the town yet,
    The grief is further down yet,
The child is *not* the model of the man that is to be.

XI.

Then come the town-pollutions :
An æon of ablutions
Shall not restore the freshness of the stream above
   the town ;
   The Arve has joined the Rhone now,
   With tardiness of flow now,
And weightier wave of water it for ever runneth
   down.

XII.

On towards the sea though !
Little does the stream know
All the wealth of wonderment awaiting it in
   death ;
   Dreams that it shall find there
   All before it found fair,
Purity of raiment, and a joy that takes the breath.

XIII.

Fullest restoration
To rightful rank and station ;
Perfected development of all the dreams of youth ;
   Even for him a May-queen,
   Fair, with eyes of grey-green,
And bloom of black-brown tresses, and the white-
   ness of the truth.

Good Friday, 1870.

II.

A BRIDAL-CHANT.

Hexameters.

Over the hills and far away, right into the home
    of the summer,
Hand in hand together they go, towards the region
    of sunset;
She, fair as a daughter of Eve; he, bright as a
    beam of Apollo,
Straight, upright as a rod, not bent and bowed
    together,
Like to the careworn men who within this fortu-
    nate island
Toil and moil for a crust, and exist, and dream
    they are living.
Fair as the sons of Greece who beneath the un-
    speakable ether
Wrought, and fought with the gods, the givers of
    might to mortals,
Givers of might and of manhood, and lust of doing
    and daring;
Givers of strength in the struggle, and endless
    perseverance.
Fair as Psyche is fair, bright, beautiful, gift of the
    goddess
(She who rewards the brave with ecstasy not to be
    uttered),
Sweet as Venus herself, was the Bride who blos-
    somed before him.

III.

THE EMIGRANT'S SONG.

Hark to the dashing of the deep blue sea
  As the sides of the boat are gleaming
Through deep-drawn furrows of the lands that are
        free,
  With a foam-line after us streaming!

Life before us, and room to expand!
  Let us steer for the home of the sunset,
Let us make for the shores of an infinite land
  And smile at the swift waves' onset.

Let us cast from off us the chains of the old
  And look to a life that is new;
As the creeds of the past wax fainter and cold,
  Clear rises a creed that is true.

We shall soon be free; far out of the reach
  Of the priests, and the tales of tradition;
Fear not: we shall ground on a gravelly beach,
  And arrive at a rightful condition.

Let us leave the churches that clamour and cry,
  And put the books on the shelves;
Come, men, my brothers, at least we will try
  To find us a faith for ourselves!

We are leaving lands where respectable saints
    Look down on the poor and the old;
Where Nature is scorned, and humanity faints,
    And women are bought and sold.

Where priests shriek shouts, and condemn their
        betters,
    While women fall faint, and fade before them,
Believing in lies, believing in fetters,
    And not in the truth of the Spirit that bore them.

The Spirit that lords it over the sea,
    Shines in the sunshine, walks in the wind,
Sounds in the life of the leaves of a tree,
    Kisses the eyes of a soul that has sinned.

Clothèd upon with the might of the thunder
    And brighter than brightness of lightning rays;
Fulfilled with life — dividing asunder
    The soul and the body, the nights and days.

The Spirit that breathes in the infinite ether,
    And clothes the night with a mantle of stars;
All-gracious; smiling on mortals beneath her;
    Spirit of peace-time, Spirit of wars.

Strong to rejoice in the roar of the battle,
    Strong to inspire the might of a man
Calm in the midst of its thunderous rattle,
    Leaping alert in the heart of the van.

Holding the threads of the life of the nations,
    Songs of the seasons, tides of the sea;
Dealing rewards and condemnations,
    Fashioning, causing to cease to be.

Bringer of birth-time, worker of wonder,
  Daily developing life in the earth ;
Maker of heat, light, forger of thunder,
  Seasons of sadness, hours of mirth.

Maker of hours of work and of playtime,
  And above all things, Author of love—
Love the incarnate spirit of May-time,
  Spirit that broods with the wings of a dove.

Love that slayeth and love that healeth,
  With the power of life and death in his wings ;
Love with the ice-cold power that congealeth,
  And love the looser of frozen strings.

Sweet love that gladdens with gleams of the
      spring-time,
  And scent of flowers, and singing of birds ;
And leaves that re-echo the lilt of the wind-
      rhyme,
  And laughter, and musical lowing of herds.

Such is the Spirit that fools are blaspheming,
  Preaching of darkness, horrors of hell,
Torturing souls who are timidly dreaming
  That *if* a God reigneth it *must* be well.

Well for the good men, well for the sinners,
  Well for the priests, whose power shall fall ;
Well for the saints and the feeble beginners ;
  Some way or other, well for us all.

IV.

THE DEAD MEN'S SONG.

I.

Praise we death
Who stays our breath
And sends us rest from pain ;
Slay we life
With edge of knife
And hurl him back again.

II.

Praise the tomb,
The utmost gloom
Of garments graveyards hold ;
The dead men's lyre,
And flames of fire
From mouth of skeleton rolled.

III.

Praise the dance
Of feet that prance
Upon the ball-room floor
Deep down below,
Where worm-buds grow,
And light's alive no more.

IV.

Slay we love,
The feeble dove,
And smear her wings with clay !
Here below
We dead men know
Her not—the beetles play.

V.

And mosses damp,
And clink of clamp,
And spiders' webs entwined
In hair of ours,
In woven bowers,
Are dear to dead men's mind.

V.

Half-eaten eyes
With no surprise
We see : that sort of thing
Is common here ;
Whole eyes are dear ;
This is the song we sing.

V.

THE WIFE'S RETURN.

Deary me, what a dirty room!
Quick, my husband, bring me a broom,
And let me sweep away the gloom
    That reigns when I'm not here.

This is the way you treat the place
When I, your wife, no longer grace
This home of ours with the light of my face—
    'Tis enough to move a tear!

Get you gone, and let me alone;
Out of the way; and when you're flown
I'll sweep it clean as if 'twere mown—
    You go and fetch the beer.

The only thing, I often think,
That the men are fit for is to drink
Or empty soap-suds into the sink:
    I'm never away but I fear;

Fear for the garden most of all,
Dream of the pigs, and hear them squall,
And see the children playing at ball
    On the flower-beds, far and near.

See the potatoes going to rot,
The peas in pieces, and what not,
The cabbages all a mouldy lot,
    And never a currant clear.

Never you mind—I'm home again,
And that's the chief thing; only when
Next time I go, be sure that then
    You manage better, dear.

VI.

GOOD-NIGHT.

Good-night, good-night!
  Till dawn of day
  May soft sleep stay
  By you, I pray;
Till breaks the light;
Good-night—good-night.

Good-night, good-night!
  The day was glad
  When you I had
  In sight, but sad
Is now my plight;
Good-night—good-night.

Good-night, good-night!
  The darkness teems
  With you : in dreams
  I hunt the gleams
Of tresses bright;
Good-night—good-night.

Good-night, good-night!
  Till to-morrow
  Sorrow—sorrow :
  Then we borrow
Wings for flight;
Good-night—good-night.

Good-night, good-night!
  I think of you,
  My hero true,
  The long night through;
Till shines the light;
Good-night—good-night.

Good-night, good-night!
  To-morrow, sweet,
  Again we meet,
  And gone the feet
Of evil plight;
Good-night—good-night.

Good-night, good-night!
  I feel your hand,
  I see you stand
  In dim dream-land,
In garments bright;
Good-night—good-night.

Good-night, good-night!
  Yours am I, sweet,
  Slow to sigh, sweet,
  Swift to fly, sweet,
Strong for flight;
Good-night—good-night.

Good-night, good-night!
   The last adieu :
   To-morrow's dew
   Will fall on two,
On love alight;
Good-night—good-night.

Good-night, good-night!
   The last kiss blown,
   The last look flown,
   From off his throne
Must love alight;
My own—good-night.

VII.

BEYOND THE YEARS!

Beyond the years there lies a compensation
   For all this heaped-up mountainous pile of woe,
   This Alpine elevation of the snow
Of sorrow, this most piteous tribulation,—
     These oceans filled at founts of women's
      tears;
For all, I tell you, waiteth compensation
   Beyond the years!

For all the agony, and heart-sick groaning,
   And agitation of uplifted hands
   That seek to pull God down from where He stands
And force His silent eyes to see the moaning,
   To listen to the heaving of the lands,
There waiteth somewhere, somehow, compen-
     sation;
   A flower expands

Of hope that beckoneth weary footsteps forward
   Towards a possibility of life,
   A possible cessation of the strife,
A possible approach of earth's ship shoreward:
As watcheth for a husband's step a wife,
   Our eyes are strained towards this compensation
   For ceaseless planetary tribulation,
   This cutting of the cord of our damnation
     With keen-edged knife.

D

TO A LILY.

SUMMER LOVE.

TO A LILY.

SUMMER LOVE.

BRUISED BLOSSOMS.

My love went—flinging from her mantle fast
  Along the dusty and forsaken road
  Strange flowers and fruits that bloomed and
    shone and glowed,
Re-lighting the pale tapers of the past,
Making the wilderness a temple vast;
  And a sweet woman, slighter but as fair,
  Went, gathering bruised blossoms in her hair,
And round about their stems her veil she cast.

• And unto me she brought the flowers and fruits,
  Weeping, and with soft pity in her eyes,
And laid her tender hand on severed roots;
  And if a bud or any petal lies
Broken, she waileth—and the sundered shoots
  To re-establish in green bloom she tries.

THE LILY AND THE ROSE.

A lily with the fragrance of my rose
   Mingled strange fleeting odours passing sweet,
   And in the imprint of that flower's feet
Left novel tints and subtle signs of snows ;
Now in my heart a double blossom blows,
   And all my soul is ravished by the heat
   Of summer twice inflamed, and seems to beat
Responsive as the ascending season grows.

For first the rose with crimson scent delayed
   The full outpouring of the lily's breath,
   And faint her presence was and pale as death,
And timidly she lingered in the shade ;
But now I kiss with valour every braid,
   And yearn ecstatic o'er each word she saith.

THE BATTLE OF FLOWERS.

Two flowers struggled hard within my soul,
   The spirits of a lily and a rose—
   And first on high the crimson odour grows,
And next a snow-white vapour seems to roll
The gates of sound asunder, and control
   My heart till song's liquescence overflows ;
   So each sweet flower alternate rules and blows,
Each in a variously fragrant stole.

But lo ! one morning when I woke I saw
   Myself adorned in smooth delicious white—
   And, wondering at the unaccustomed sight
Of such a body made devoid of flaw,
Perceived myself with deep unuttered awe
   Clothed in the lily's plumes from left to right.

CRIMSON AND MANY FLOWERS.

" I loved another blossom," so I said—
   " And she was somewhat fairer, sweet, than
      you ; "
The maiden answered not, but closer drew
The tender-shielding bounty of her head,
And in that moment lo ! one love was dead
   And golden wings proclaimed a goddess new,
   And as her pinions fluttered into view
The sun was risen turbulent and red—
   The vehement approach of a new day
That shall surpass the former, and outshine
   With a supreme unparalleled display
Those weeping misty seasons that were mine,
And round about my rugged brows shall twine
   Crimson and many flowers for thorns and grey.

A WOMAN'S BLOOM.

"My heart hath suffered, sweet one:" But she
   brought
  The nearer that down-bending, gracious head,
  And, though no word articulate was said,
That tender token hath a marvel wrought,
A miracle of healing beyond thought—
  For on a lonely grave a rose was red
  That moment, and a crimson heart that bled
Was stanched and white, and ceased to suffer
    aught :—

And over me there flowed a wealth of hair,
  And that strange endless unforeseen perfume
Was subtle and abundant in the air—
  The fire that scorches but doth not consume,
  The sweet outpouring of a woman's bloom,
Unutterably wonderful and fair.

PARTING.

PARTING.

THOSE SUMMER NIGHTS.

When we were happy in those summer nights,
   Making great London but a soft green wood
   As each beside the other silent stood,
Breathing a mutual nosegay of delights,
We were not conscious of love's present heights—
   But now, possession being cold and thin,
   With no sweet golden lovers' gate to win,
We recognise and eulogise love's rights.

"Ah! that was sweet"—so each may sob and say—
   "That evening when glad August in the trees
   And shrubs made such a tender lovers' breeze : "
For, visible from an October grey,
The past is as a gold transfigured day,
   The present as the sapless nights that freeze.

SWEET FANCY'S HAND.

It is sweet fancy's hand that crowns the past—
  For, when we were together, you and I,
  The ground was dull and motionless and dry,
Across it a wan veil of colour cast;
Now, swept by my imagination's blast,
  It glitters like a countless summer sky,
  And round about our feet the flowers fly,
And wings of birds succeed each other fast.

For every step we took I see a flower
  Bloom in the dreary desert of the squares,—
  The arid pasture of our London airs
Is even as a sweet rose-planted bower,
And every spot we lingered in an hour
  An endless flood of vegetation bears.

A FAR-OFF HILL.

Ah, sweet, now you are gone, I see the days
  We spent together, colourless before,
  Flame with triumphant lustre more and more,
Till every street we threaded is a blaze
Of splendour, and the sad dust-stricken ways
  Shine as a moon-enamoured silver shore ;
  My fancy brings each tone of yours of yore,
And every smile, into my weeping gaze.

It always is so : as a sun-kissed hill
  Shines in the distance, girt about with fear
And mystery, whose beauty could not fill
  The over-daring eye when we were near,
So gleams a far-off passion,—soft and still
  And awful, and unutterably clear.

WITH WHITER PLUMES.

I loved a lily : The sweet flower was near,
   And, bearing petals less majestic far,
   Shone as a lesser individual star,
Made by a sweet proximity as dear
As the imperial rose,—and white and clear
   The lily shone; but when the flower was full,
   Another hand had interfered to pull
The petals,—an intruder's foot was here.

And so I miss my lily and my rose,
   Fated to love for ever but to find
No flower for me her tenderest depths disclose ;
   Yet bear I some triumphant mirth of mind,
   In that the lily kissed me, and hath shined
Because of me with whiter plumes of snows.

LOVE AND HONOUR.

I stood before a grave,—and honour said,
   " Heap loudly on the corpse that lies therein
   Dust and departure—that the soul may win
The eternal halo of a passion dead,
And round about her lips for roses red
   Twine lilies pale as her own life hath been ;
   And seize thine harp, sad singer, and begin
Some low-voiced tune to tears and yearning wed."

But love said, " Rather let the corpse awake !
   And let sweet lips for.roses be the charm
   To bring towards an unhesitating arm
The tender limbs and soft desires that shake
And flutter as a lily for thy sake—
   Even as a lily loud in her alarm."

———————

E

THE MAGIC OF MEMORY.

I.

When you were *with* me, sweet, I could not lead
  Your presence through the corridors of rhyme :
  But you are smitten by the snows of time,
And by swift disappointment's sword I bleed,
And, having chosen an unselfish creed,
  In every flowery avenue of mind
  A gracious footprint of my love's I find,
And sonnets spring by thousands out of seed !

Before I lost you, I was silent,—now
  That I have given you into other hands,
  The gardens of my brain are tuneful lands,
And linnets twitter round about my brow,
And nightingales are loud on every bough,
  And thrushes chant your praise in laughing
    bands.

II.

The roads we trod together, gleam and shine,—
  Grey, cold, and sour, and flint-bedecked before,—
  But now the moon of fancy on the shore
Of bitter absence sheds a silver line,

And, as the gossamer-woven webs combine
   To elude our present overpowering tread,
   But flame in sweet prismatic green and red
And gold and fairy lacework clean and fine
   When distance has transfigured the broad field—
So every stone we touched in this dull town,
Then garbed in ordinary dust and brown,
   A golden flash of colour seems to yield,
   And shines like some anointed luscious shield,
Under the bitter fire of memory's frown.

WINTER LOVE.

WINTER LOVE.

THIS AFTERNOON.

This afternoon I go to meet my love,—
 And, through the earlier moments of the day,
 My pulses like swift throbbing surges play,
Mixed with the soft respiring of a dove,
And pinions beat the azure cliffs above
 And frolic in and out each windy bay—
 I triumph ; for she hath not answered " Nay ;"
I hold her written word in sign thereof.

Ah, love ! 'tis but a wintry afternoon,
 Yet will we make it as a summer sleep
 Winged with strange odours passing soft and
 deep—
A clear and passionate crimson-hooded swoon :
And though our ruddy heaven be over soon,
 It leaves a rose for either heart to keep.

A SUN-GOD.

Soon thou shalt lay thy tender hands on me
   And the strong force of passion shall ignite,.
   Struck as a sudden comet into light
By the inviting flame of love I see
Bloom as a crimson mantle over thee—
   Even as the snows below the hills are white,
   But next the Alpine sun shine red and bright,
Rosy for miles upon the mountain-knee.

Yea, thou shalt change me from a quiet star,
   Following the universal rounded road,
Desiring thee in silence from afar,
   Into a sun-god,—bearing the white load
Of thy sweet misty body in a car
   Of flame towards some desirable abode.

A TALISMAN.

I have not seen you,—and the days have been
  But as a meagre and remorseful time,
  The likeness of some frozen blue-clad clime,
Some destitute abode of tears and sin ;
But summer is upon us, and we win
  The roses and the dreams of mute delight
  That clothe the sweet limbs of a summer night,.
And hem the fragrant arms of summer in.

Summer is as a fragrant rose-plumed bird,
  Young, and delirious with its own desire ;
  Winter is as a worn-out aged fire—
But somewhere of a talisman I heard
That hath the magic potency to gird
  Roses about each wintry wan-built briar.

LOVE'S CRUELTY.

Sweet, every meeting-time may be our last !
 We stand upon time's beach, and, after, one
 May launch a boat with cunning keel to run
Against the sidelong pressure of the blast,
With curved resistance of a reedlike mast,
 Into the hollows of the western sun—
 Time finished, red eternity begun,
Our love may be but as a rosebud past,
 Crying in some disastrous nook of garden
After the heels of summer, who declares,
 Invincible and destitute of pardon,
His lips are languid for Australian airs,—
And, with love's endless cruelty, prepares
 The alternate hemisphere to inflame and harden.

I SEND A SONG.

This afternoon I am to meet you, sweet.
  The torrents of my longing overflow,
  As from white clouds descending streams of
    snow
Cover with feathery flakes our halting feet :
I send a song in front of me to meet
  The soft advancing rosebud-lips I know
  So truly, that I think I see them grow
With increase soft and odorous and fleet.

Song ! lay upon her lips my panting soul
  Already in advance of this slow clock,
  That it may sway from side to side, and rock
Even as a flower floating in a bowl
Upon those fragrant billowy tides, the whole
  Of which shall overwhelm me when I knock.

AND SHALL I SEE YOU?

And shall I see you, sweet, and are you still
  Soft and as white and gentle as before?
  And doth the moon still beam along the shore
With tender eyes and yellow rays that thrill
The pebbles and the yearning foam, and spill
  Their passionate effulgence more and more?
  Sweet, thou shalt lay thine hand upon the sore
Heart-spot of parting, and thine eyes shall fill
  The cup of my strong being till it yearns
And trembles into air and overflows:
  Even as the sun's imperious mandate turns
The bending face and body of a rose
Upward—till every petal doth unclose,
  Blushing, and every vein and fibre burns.

WHERE THOU ART, SWEET.

Where thou art, sweet, it matters not to know
  Whether sweet summer's sceptre reigns supreme,
  For thou art girded with a luscious dream
That darts a rosy radiance over snow,
As thou dost tread triumphant to and fro,—
  The light wherewith thy winged feet do teem;
  Where they have trodden, the amorous grasses
    seem
To blossom into flame and overflow,
  As at the advent of twin goddesses;
And, when thy hand is laid upon my neck,
  It is even as a shower divine to bless
The solemn marble, cleansed from every fleck
By the descending silvery flames that check
  The thunders of sin's turbulent distress.

EVEN AS THE DOVE.

Even as the dove went, errant from the ark,
   Speeding with hopeful pinions through the deep
   To analyse the awful void, and peep
If anywhere a green and living spark
Her eyes of bright intelligence might mark—
   Fly, fragrant-winged song, towards my love,
   Dividing with the white breast of a dove
The inanimate resistance of the dark.

Seek her, and hover over her in spite
   Of the dark-panoplied adulterous storm,
And seize from off her lips a rosebud white,
   Tender and irreproachable and warm,—
   And hasten with that soft inviolate form
Through the wild ebbing armies of the night.

1871.

ODE TO ENGLAND.

STROPHE I.

At length the lands arise
With heaven-seeking eyes ;
No more they search the past,
And backward glances cast
Towards fields of Galilee
And that blue inland sea :
But every land adores
The God of its own shores,
The Deity of its hills,
The Spirit of its rills,
Redeemer of its plains,
Who o'er its cities reigns
Cleansing each soul from stains.

STROPHE II.

Lift up your eyes towards the morning brightness,
　Dwell no more 'mid the past like sons of slaves :
Lo ! even here shines the exceeding whiteness
　Of Venus 'mid the surging crowns of waves,
　And Jesus rises from ten thousand graves.

The heroes of high history of each nation
   Speak in the burning records of the race;
Through wrongs, through woes, through speech-
     less tribulation,
   They sought the living God's great changeless
     face
   And now they shine star-saviours in each
     place.

Bright are their eyes and deathless is their
     glory;
   Lift up your eyes to their eyes all ye lands!
Yea, every nation, listen to the story
   Of those who moulded it with iron hands,
   And loosed its dim primeval swaddling-bands.

STROPHE III.

O England, dwell no longer
   'Mid shows of things, and dreams:
Rise, for thou art the stronger!
   Thy sunrise o'er thee beams
   And round about thee streams.

Stronger thou art and fairer
   Than lands thou hast obeyed:
Thine azure heavens are rarer;
   Why art thou thus afraid?
   Why lingerest in the shade?

Hast thou no spirits diviner
 Than Jesus, Moses, Paul ?
Art thou content with minor
 Slow-sandalled feet that crawl,
 Not fly—that stumble, fall ?

Hast thou no hearts that carry
 A yearning force supreme ?
Must thou for ever tarry,
 Possessed by some pale dream,
 While past thee nations stream ?

Rise ! greater than the immortal
 . Spirits of Greece and Rome
Thou hast within thy portal :
 Within the ring of foam
 That girds thine island-home.

STROPHE IV.

England ! bring thou blossoms from all thy hills ;
Wreathe thou tender lilies from sides of rills
Golden, flowing through vales that plenty fills.

Golden crowns of the corn, and crowns of red
Autumn leaves for the new God's kingly head
Bring thou ; he needs a wreath, for his wreaths
  are dead.

Dead are the Jewish wreaths, and the flowers of
  Rome :
Now God plunges his feet deep in the English
  foam,
Seeking this land for rest, craving a Western home.

F

Wilt thou hound him away, shriek him away
    from thee ?
Hurl him wandering forth over the barren sea ?
Build him a temple rather, marble in purity.

Let God rest and dream, hidden in thy deep meads,
Hidden and wreathed in flowers, soothing the brow
    that bleeds
Yet from the spears and thorns, finding delight
    he needs.

Here is a land for a God ; fair in body and soul.
England, give to thy God body and heart,—thy
    whole
Measureless splendid might, as of tides that
    round thee roll.

STROPHE V.

Lo ! in tender accents, hark ! the high God
    speaks ;
England, let his message flush thy languid
    cheeks !
Give to him the great gift that his longing seeks.

Give to him thy children, fair and strong and free,
Pure and brave and happy, splendid flowers of thee,
Give to him thy manhood, thy maturity.

"Weary am I," God saith, " of the pallid past ;
Brace me, wind of England, after burning blast
O' the arid Eastern deserts, where my soul was
    cast.

"Now I turn me Northward : shall I find a race
Fit to stand before me, unabashed of face?
Shall I find in England home and dwelling-
    place ? "

ANTISTROPHE I.

Doth England hear and turn
With longing eyes that yearn
And sparkle at the voice
Of Deity, and rejoice?
Or doth she, cowed and pale,
Hidden beneath the veil
Of her own feebleness,
Tremble at the stress
And force of fiery sound
That girdled her around
When the high God spoke,
And thunderlike he broke
The silence, and she woke.

ANTISTROPHE II.

Wilt thou with ferns and flowers from deep dim
    valleys
Weave a divine sweet frontlet for thy king,
O England ; now thy soul his trumpet rallies,
    What wilt thou in thine arms, O England,
      bring ?
    Wherewith wilt thou the eternal forehead
      ring ?

The bay-leaves wilt thou bind of all thy singers
Around the eternal forehead broad and white,
Touching with wŏmanly and reverent fingers
    The brow, the eyes of marvellous sweet
      light :
    Then wilt thou bring rose-crowns of lovers
      bright ?

Oh, most of all, be thine own self, and ring
    him
    With thine own strengthened and victorious
      soul :
This chiefest of all gifts, O England, bring
    him !
    Mingle in love's clear sacrificial bowl
    The wine of thine own heart made flawless,
      whole.

ANTISTROPHE III.

Let love at length its mission
    In thine own home fulfil :
Let love's sweet utmost vision
    Of perfect soul and will
    All devious passions still.

Let love at length be chainless ;
    So shall love be supreme,
Then for the first time stainless,
    A golden sunrise-gleam
    Upon a golden stream.

Pour through thine own dear meadows,
  England, one burst of song,
Scattering pain's shadows
   And all the black-plumed throng
   Of sorrows, strange and strong.

Meet, utterly white, fearless,
  The God who for thee pines :
Glad, sighless, pangless, tearless,
   Casting aside the signs
   Of suffering he divines.

Thine immemorial sorrow
  He knoweth, and shall slay :
Lo! crimson dawns the morrow
   Of many a mournful day
   Through centuries grim and grey.

ANTISTROPHE IV.

Not the dreams of the past, of the days of old,
God needs : not strange dreams of the walls of
    gold
In heaven and jewels and pearls and treasure un-
    told.

Not these things ; but the breath of the English
    air
And blossoms of spring from dells where ferns are
    fair
And jewels of star-white petals than pearls more
    rare.

And jewels of glances bright and tender and grey
Better to God now, dearer, than star-like ray
Of glances piercing the cloudless Eastern day.

And weapons of strong men's arms from the
    Northern plains
Whereover the future's sun, now rising, reigns ;
Rich armour of fearless countless hearts for his
    fanes.

These and the sound of our seas by day by night,
The limitless organ-peal of breakers white
Thrilling the new-found heart of God with might.

And the utter strength of the soul : this God re-
    quires ;
And all the worship and music of English lyres
And worship of limitless sea-like hearts he de-
    sires.

ANTISTROPHE V.

Lo ! with brave sweet accents England turns to
    thee
Great God of the past world, king now of the sea
Girding her white cliffs, lord of futurity.

"Take my thousand meadows; take each hill and
    plain ;"
So saith England : "over free glad spirits reign ;
Rule till as my seas are, souls are clear of stain.

" Pour thy kingly presence through the throbbing
    land :
Sons of God by thousands shall before thee stand
Holding daughters of thee by the white, white
    hand.

" Sons of God and daughters, saviours, shalt thou
    find
In the race thou choosest; leaders of mankind,
Voiced as are the surges, winged as is the wind."

EPODE.

Beyond the faintest region of stars or skies
Lo! England pierces the future with sunbright
    eyes.

Great spirits beyond the spirits who crowned the
    past
Shall lift the future towards summits unreached
    and vast.

Already the sound of their feet at the doors is
    heard
And the wide land shakes and quakes at their loud
    first word.

Christ-men, Christ-women, whose feet at the
    bright doors stand
Shall lift and redeem and heal and deliver the
    land.

The God in their eyes shall pierce through the
    lessening gloom
And their splendour of heart shall be treasure and
    flame and perfume.

And the places waste shall blossom, the wild ways
    sing
At the message of peace and redemption and joy
    they bring.

These England bearing thou shalt stand forth as
    a queen
And rule the future, triumphant and great of
    mien.

And God in thy waves and upon thy hills shall
    sound
And in women's souls and in men's with God's
    kiss crowned.

TO THEE, SWEET.

The music of thy song, sweet,
   Has sounded through the night:
Its accents pure and strong, sweet,
   Its fervour calm and bright,
Have lifted me along, sweet,
   Have brought God's heaven in sight.

I rested on the sound, sweet,
   With happy eyes closed fast:
Its tender magic bound, sweet,
   My soul; its glory cast
A golden veil around, sweet,—
   It changed the weary past.

I hear the song by night, sweet,
   I hear it in the day:
At dawn of soft-grey light, sweet,
   It shines upon my way;
Ever its flame in sight, sweet,
   Leads, like some heaven-sent ray.

Oh, I will try, my own sweet,
   To be to thee the flower
Thou singest of; my tone, sweet,
   With woman's tender power
Shall soothe—thou shalt be shown, sweet,
   Love's deepest rose-hung bower!

And in that bower of joy, sweet,
   Thy sorrows kissed away,
Shall pain not nor annoy, sweet;
   My heart in thine shall stay:
Love's pleasure shall not cloy, sweet,
   Nor bloom of love decay.

I dreamed a tender dream, sweet,—
   I tell it to thee here;
But the pure, gracious theme, sweet,
   Is only for thine ear:
It was a sunrise-gleam, sweet,
   Beautiful, noble, clear.

I dreamed I came to thee, sweet,—
   All barriers slipped away:
All raiment fell from me, sweet,
   I was as white as day;
I laughed in utter glee, sweet,
   More glad than I can say!

All raiment earthly melted
   Away in that fair dream:
Alone with beauty belted,
   O lover, I did seem!
I stood by thee and felt it
   Sweet, sweet,—a heaven-gleam!

Naked I stood for thee, sweet,—
   Divinely white and pure:
God clothed with passion me, sweet;
   But all that could obscure
And hinder soft love, He, sweet,
   Stripped with a mandate sure.

So all my beauty came, sweet,—
  Is it so much indeed ?
About thee like a flame, sweet,
  Thy blossom, yea thy meed ;
I had no thought of shame, sweet,
  I knew what love decreed.

I passed into thy form, sweet,
  Just like a soft, soft breeze,
A dear leaf-shaking storm, sweet,
  That laughs amid the trees :
White, tender, loving, warm, sweet,—
  White as the white, white seas.

I rushed into thine arms, sweet,
  I rushed into thy soul :
Dead was each fear that harms, sweet,
  I saw love's sacred whole
Revealed : now nought alarms, sweet,—
  I've read love's deepest scroll.

I passed with perfect peace, sweet,
  Into a life quite new :
From bondage to release, sweet,
  A freedom won by you :
Past pangs and sorrows cease, sweet,—
  I sing, glad in the blue.

I sing for very gladness,
  I, who was once afraid|:
I, who once in deep sadness
  Sat, as in dark damp glade ;
I, who have met grim madness,
  And longed to sip night-shade.

I sing ; for thou hast won me,
 Sweet lover, poet, king :
Thy loving soul hath spun me
 Soft wedding-raiment ; ring
Of genius given, and done me
 Proud honour ; so I sing.

I come to thee in dreaming,
 I come in waking thought :
When fancies swift are streaming
 Throughout me, clasped and caught
In golden network gleaming,
 I come : such dreams I've brought !

I come on earth ; in heaven,
 Sweet love, I'll come the more :
When earth's worn garb is riven
 And on the eternal shore
Life's bark is tossed and driven,
 My love at last I'll pour

In utter perfect power, sweet,
 Upon thee ! thou shalt know
What pleasure love can shower, sweet,
 What woman's hand can throw
Of magic round her bower, sweet—
 How woman's heart can glow !

I'll come to thee at last, sweet,
 And be thy very queen ;
A whisper on the blast, sweet,
 A crown of starry sheen :
I'll give thee all my past, sweet,
 Its storms, its hours serene.

I'll give thee the old loves, sweet,
  Such as the old loves were !
Lead thee through former groves, sweet,
  Wherein, not all unfair,
The former singing doves, sweet,
  Sang,—in the youthful air.

I'll give thee all the wonder
  Of sweet, sweet youthful days :
Delight at wild stern thunder,
  Joy in the lightning-blaze ;
The past, the now, the yonder,
  In one glad wreath I raise.

I come to thee a girl, sweet,
  Long ere my mother died,
And bring thee a pale curl, sweet,
  Cut when I left her side:
Better than gold or pearl, sweet,—
  A gift of me thy bride !

The great strange billows hoary
  I saw by childhood's seas
I bring thee, and the glory
  Of myriad forest trees ;
Yea, all the pure life-story
  Learned at my mother's knees.

My sorrows and my prayers, sweet,
  My groaning and my tears,
The balm of summer airs, sweet,
  Hopes, agonies, and fears ;
All these your strong soul shares, sweet,
  Yea, all the long, long years !

The years before we met, sweet,
  Before dear passion spoke,
And tender eyes were wet, sweet,
  And love his golden yoke
Upon our shoulders set, sweet,
  And all the old fetters broke.

I give thee all these things, sweet;
  My body and my soul
My utter passion brings, sweet,—
  Myself: I give the whole.
I've got no golden wings, sweet,
  No nectared honeyed bowl.

But womanhood's dear whiteness
  Of body, spirit, mind,
And lips of untouched brightness,
  And faithfulness thou'lt find!
Oh, love hath perfect rightness,
  And sweetly all designed!

Oh, take me: hold me close, sweet,
  I'm but a woman's soul,
A clinging woman-rose, sweet,
  Whose tendrils round thee stole
To find in thee repose sweet,
  Love, husband, heaven-joy, goal!

YEARNING.

Sad are all we to think
  Of sorrows, and wasted lives
  In the dim great towns, in the hives
  Of the people; for one that thrives,
How many lost souls sink,
  Sink each day, do you think?

Why does He not stay His hand,
  God, who knows of it all?
  Was He strong to slacken the thrall
  Of the Jews, and Jericho's wall
To shake for a Hebrew band—
  Shortened for us is His hand?

If we are too many, we protest;
  If we are too many for His eye
  To cover, for Him to espy,
  Let us cease to be, let us die;
Let us sink in the sea to our rest,
  And cease not, dying, to protest.

To protest against high God who made
  More souls than His hands could keep,
  Who holdeth our sad tears cheap,
  And agony all we reap,
The reward with which we are paid,
  We, whom alive He has made.

But, if He has not forgotten
  Any whom His hands have made,
  And no one, of all men, has strayed
  From His sight ; if He covers with His shade
Each of us, by Him begotten,
  It is well, our torment is stayed.

Here, upon earth, it is wrong
  For a father to leave his child
  Without a provision ; less mild
  Than a mother is God who has smiled
The world into being ? we are strong,
  Were it so, to say it is wrong.

Surely, in His hand, for each
  Hidden, must our God have in store
  Gifts He is willing to outpour,
  Waiting, and willing, and more ;
Waiting till He can reach
  With His own, the hand of each.

Waiting until each cries
  For his Father, and looks to His hand ;
  Then will His bounty expand,
  And silent deserts of sand
Beneath sun, beneath blue sweet skies,
  Shall be changed to a green glad land.

1870.

A FAREWELL TO POETRY.

I take within mine hand
The relics of the land
Of dreams and songs and hopes and fair past
  glory;
I gather all the past
And round about it cast
A mistlike robe of soft remembrance hoary;
My singing days I bind
Together, and swift wind
In one the golden threads of life's fast-deepening
  story.

Dear blossoms, roses red,
That once about my head
Waved with a flood of soft caressing splendour,
I bid you all farewell;
Yea, to each flower that fell
Upon youth's brows from heaven with flower-
  touch tender;
A long goodbye to all—
White roses, lilies tall;
I would not fail to one sweet final thanks to
  render.

O ferns and meadow-sweet,
O rivulets that beat
With silvery footing once amid the grasses,
A long, long, long goodbye!
O many a sunset sky,
O giant purple clouds in heaped-up masses,
O seas that climbed and surged,
By wintry storm-blasts urged,
Farewell—ere from you all my mortal vision passes!

Goodbye, goodbye, goodbye—
Blue perfect summer sky,
And all the dreams of youth and hopes that
wandered
Towards heaven on sun-bright wings:
A new chant in me rings,
And gone are the old ecstasies I pondered;
Farewell, ye high designs,
The wreath that manhood twines
Is better than the leaves youth wildly plucked and
squandered.

O happy days of song
That, when my heart was strong,
Brought me life's holiest rest and sweetest treasure,
For ever, now, farewell:
The silent time-waves swell,
And their foam-crests no man can pass or measure
Beyond the singing days,
Beyond the need of bays,
Urge me—towards death's sublime unidle wakeful
leisure.

To those who love, I leave
What my hand doth achieve
·Of passionate pure love-praise and worthy singing :
The lovers who shall come
When this my voice is dumb
Shall hear in song faint echoes of it ringing,
And I shall seem to be
In heaven or on the sea,
·Or in the blossoms round their ladies' white
brows clinging.

Oh, am I not a part
Of England's songful heart,
And can I pass and be no more a token ?
Shall not the lovers young
To whom my soul hath sung
Hear by my chant the summer silence broken ?
Shall not some girlish heart
Tremble and bound and start,
As if a real live voice some sudden word had
spoken ?

I cannot wholly die
If from the blue dear sky
I bend in gracious song above true lovers ;
If in the forest deep
Among the leaves I sleep,
And murmur 'mid the green, close-foliaged covers ;
If o'er the eternal sea
Some sign and speech of me
In the wide track of pure mysterious moonlight
hovers.

If in my city too,
London made great and new,
My voice is heard, though I am gone for ever;
If lovers, in my town,
My singing for a crown
Wear, then as the red sunset ceaseth never,
I too shall never cease,
Nor dwindle nor decrease,
Nor from my well-loved streets my spirit-presence
sever.

So, farewell, lovers all!
Around me once I call
The well-known English flowers and English faces:
On every side of me
Dear blossoms I would see
Once more, sweet petals plucked from all loved
places;
And round me once again
The glad strong looks of men
My friends I'd meet,—and eyes whose light all
sorrow chases.

Sweet eyes of love once more
Upon me, as before,
Glance tenderly, lift once again long lashes!
And, ocean, once more sound,
And blossoms, once abound,
For every flower some pang of death abases!
And, lyre of mine, one song
In death's teeth, clear and strong
Cast,—ere death's conquering tide across my
heart-strand dashes!

Then let me pass from life,
And song and love and strife,
Content, my labour done, my soul not fearing;
Not doubting that I go
Towards regions where the glow
Of sunset on our mountains disappearing
Is a new rose-red day
On grander peaks than they,
Peaks which my ardent swift fatigueless foot
is nearing.

TO ELLA DIETZ: POET AND ACTRESS.

I.

O dark-eyed singer
And soft sweet bringer
Of dreams that haunt us with dear white wings,
Singer that comest
From far and hummest
The tune new to us that through thee rings,
Lift us we pray thee,
From day to day thee
Seeking, as round us thy soft soul clings.

II.

In new sweet glowing
Soft numbers flowing
Sing to us of lands we ne'er have known ;
Of rivers whose tides
Lave measureless sides
And lakes that put to the shame our own,
And forests gigantic,
And breathe the Atlantic
Upon us in song, by the great winds blown.

III.

Thou bringest for dower
A new world's power
And thine own beauty of voice and heart ;
    Gifted as thou,
    With the genius-brow,
Why shouldst thou ever retreat, depart ?
    Stay with us rather
    Sweet one, and gather
Crowns for thy young head, crowns for thine Art.

IV.

Gather the flowers
Here growing from bowers
Wherein thy young fair feet shall tread ;
    Lo ! England's pages
    From far strange ages
Yearn for thee, burn for thee, wait to be read ;
    The might of our race
    Shall flame in thy face
And gird thee and arm thee and ring thine head.

V.

Thou comest to add
Thine own soul glad
Or sorrowful sometimes unto the few
    Great women who live
    With us ever and give
Their hearts so tender, so sweet of hue,
    To the ages, to bless,
    To heal and redress,
Whose souls are as song-birds heard in the blue.

VI.

At seasons a queen
Immortal, serene,
Is sent by Apollo to lift and delight :
Her golden hair
Is his fetter, his snare,
And it draws by its glory, allures by its might;
For a season she stands
With his harp in her hands
And we mark in her eyes the god's glance bright.

VII.

So is it with thee :
From over the sea
Thou comest a new song bringing, divine;
The god in thine eyes
As the sun in the skies,
And the voice of the god in the sound of thy
rhyme;
Black-haired, Apollo
The gold-haired follow
Towards heights yet grander, peaks more sublime.

VIII.

With self-denial,
Through pain, through trial,
The high god follow, and work his will:
Not those he chooses
Whom pain refuses
To crown,—not such doth the high god thrill;
Yea, those who would follow
The steps of Apollo
Must face the night-wind bitter and shrill.

IX.

Not in the daylight,
Fickle and gay light,
Are high crowns fashioned, and great songs sung :
    Lo ! through the starlight
    The gold-haired far light
Apollo is seen and his voice hath rung
    Beneath the moonlight,
    Breathing a tune light
Which round the red lips eddied and clung.

X.

If thou wilt find him,
Seize and wilt bind him,
High up the mountains, beneath the stars,
    Follow thou fearless ;
    The rough rocks cheerless
Traverse and heed not the moist fresh scars ;
    High in the azure
    Thou shalt have pleasure,
Beyond all limits, above all bars.

XI.

But few can follow
King-god Apollo ;
And of these singers, of women how few
    There have been truly
    Who faithfully, duly,
The great god served and his greatness knew ;
    Wilt thou make over
    As bard, as lover,
Thy soul to the song-god, canst thou be true ?

XII.

Yea, true for ever,
Though gladdened never
By voice delusive of fluctuant praise
Of dim-souled hearer ;
Oh how far clearer
Ring out Apollo's own splendid lays !
The sun-god's kiss,
Thou mayest have *this*,
The sun-god's lips, and the song-god's bays.

XIII.

Lift up thy spirit,
Make thine and inherit
Our land's past story, our country's calm ;
Let our seas gladden thee,
Our sorrows sadden thee,
Our summers soothe thee with waft of balm ;
Our winters brace thee,
Our hearts encase thee
As thou our roses within thy palm.

XIV.

Let every flower
In every bower
Of England greet thee with upturned face ;
Rose and each lily
And hair-bell hilly
And delicate snowdrop's maiden grace ;
And snow-drop girls
With golden curls
Brought for thy welcome from many a place.

XV.

Thy voice shall reach us,
Thine heart shall teach us
Of things we know not : thy lyre shall sound
By the great white surges
The North wind urges
With terrible glee, as it shakes the ground ;
And in our summer
O sweet new-comer
Thy softer songs shall laugh and abound.

XVI.

Thyself a flower
Thy pure scent shower
O fair flower-singer about our shore :
A new scent tender
Of new strange splendour,
Sweet as the scents were gathered of yore
From the harp-swaying fingers
Of some three singers
Who sang the song-god's altar before.

XVII.

Some three or four,
Apollo no more
Took pains to nurture nor cared to crown :
They passed away from us
And took the day from us,
And all the leaves of our life were brown,
And autumn came
And the dead year's shame
At their departure and cold death's frown.

XVIII.

Now, dark-eyed chanter,
Be giver, be granter
Of new spring to us; bid England's plains
At thy sweet footing
Awake, forth-shooting
New green shafts as at the soft spring-rains
Bid summer blossoms
Ope bright glad bosoms,
And violets peep in the moist moss-lanes.

XIX.

Arising later,
Thou shalt be greater
Than many and many who came and sang
Till the high hills sounded
As songs abounded,
And the echoing sea-waves laughed and **they rang:**
Thou shalt step higher,
With more sweet fire
Within thy spirit, more pure song-pang.

XX.

Not bay-leaves olden
But his own golden
Dear locks Apollo shall bend and twine
Within thy dark,
Like many a spark
Of flame-flies floating, let loose in thine:
And an English rose
In the dark hair glows
To render it ever and ever divine.

TO KATHLEEN GORDON,
GIRL-GENIUS.

I.

O girl-soul tender,
And girl-form slender,
What dreams have traversed from side to side
Thy young fair being,
Beyond our seeing—
What thoughts have smitten with wing-wafts wide
The moonlit ocean
Of hopes in motion,
Around thee surging in life's first pride.

II.

Dreaming for ever,
Despairing never,
How beautiful art thou, spirit divine!
A blossom in girl-shape,
Purer than pearl-shape,
Born upon earth as a rose to shine;
Born to deliver
The souls that quiver
From arrows of life as from salt sea-brine.

III.

Born to delight us
With song-beams that smite us,
Calm, gladden us, heal us—dreaming of things
That men dream never
And reach not ever
With masculine strong stern struggle of wings;
Teacher of poet,
Thou dost not know it,
But sweet within thee our song-god sings.

IV.

Sings, and he brings to us
Tender soft wings, to us
Showing delights new, found not of old;
In thy light fairy
Dear diction airy
The song-god speaks and his speech is of gold,
And he laughs in laughter
Of thine, and, after,
He clings to us, sings to us, gentle but bold.

V.

Thou wast a flower
In some dim bower
Of Paradise, doubt not; now thou art here
To sing for years to us,
Laughter and tears to us,
Spread forth thy pinions, and have no fear;
The airs will carry thee,
Thy genius marry thee
In thought to spirits whose songs are clear.

VI.

Whose songs are tender,
Grave, and of splendour
Divine in ages long past and dead :
Shelley shall sing to thee
And Keats' soul cling to thee ;
For robe and raiment, to crown thine head,
Thou shalt have glory
Of ages hoary,
The singing of past days round thee shed.

VII.

Hold to thy power
O girl, O flower,
Both firm and humble, both true and brave ;
Hearts thou shalt gladden,
Some souls perhaps sadden,
But more deliver and heal and save ;
Add to our pleasure
With thy sweet treasure
Of fancies bountiful, frolick or grave.

VIII.

Twine for our meadows
Sunbeams and shadows
Of delicate true song, as in the strain
Thou just hast given us,
Whose dart hath riven us
Wondering to find in the song-god's fane
So young a singer,
So sweet a bringer
Of gifts that only the young flowers gain.

IX.

For only the singers,
Young, sweet, are bringers
Of all that falls from the high god's hand;
Yea, such souls only,
Pure, wondrous, lonely,
Before Apollo uncrowned, crowned, stand;
Crowned not as older
Bards fiercer or colder,
But crowned with rosebuds, band upon band.

X.

Not e'en with bay-leaves,
Sorrow's dark stray leaves,
But only rosebuds bright as the morn,
Bright as thine own heart;
Just as thou blown art
Yesterday only, so these were born
Yesterday, sweet one,
Subtle and fleet one—
From rose-twigs for thee were plucked and torn.

XI.

Thy white brow bears yet
No sign of cares, yet
Some sorrow thy song would seem to pour;
Thou hast within thee
Strange thoughts that win thee,
Lure thee and draw thee to lands before;
To seasons unseen yet,
Cloudless, serene yet,
Towards passions the years yet garner in store.

XII.

O girl-heart dreaming
Of gold hair gleaming
And anthems swelling, and dark bright eyes,
Thy young life coming,
Like far wings humming
Above the blossoms 'neath sunstruck skies,
Hints of its wonder
Breathes—in the thunder
Of night, and the light of moons that rise.

XIII.

A flower thou blowest,
Just that,—nor knowest
The strange lands shadowed thy feet shall tread;
Best that thou know not,
While such skies glow not,
Fierce, sultry, scorching, above thine head;
The sunrise over thee
Shields, like a lover, thee;
What knowst thou, child-heart, of sunset red?

XIV.

Thou needst not linger
Pale sweet girl-singer
As yet, nor ponder by death's dark streams;
Yet, in thy singing
Their ripples ringing
Surge upward slowly, and softest dreams
Pour through thy yearning
Heart bounding and burning,
And crown thy spirit with weird sad gleams.

H

XV.

Dreams thou hast fashioned,
Tender, impassioned,
Of death, of heaven, of things unseen;
But wings supremer
O dear girl-dreamer
Than angels' even shall o'er thee lean;
Love's plumes shall crown thee,
In sweet joy drown thee,
Ere death thou facest, soft and serene.

XVI.

Ere death thou facest
In love's thou placest
Thy palm so trustful and towards love's eyes
Thou gazest upward
As heaven and hopeward,
As towards star-blazoned and spotless skies:
Not for us only
The young song lonely
On lonely wing-beats glitters and flies.

XVII.

Thou shalt be flower
In love's fair hour
To those we see not—to him we see
Not either; lady
Now 'neath the shady
Dear branches supple of youth's slim tree
Resting, and singing
The soft songs clinging
To girl-friends' spirits, to many, to me.

XVIII.

But dream thou onward
Moonward and sunward,
Starward and seaward, skyward,—and hold
Dear, dear, the flowing
Locks, golden, glowing,
Thy sweet songs tell of,—for nought but gold
Thou wilt, thou sayest;
Thy voice delayest
Never for black locks, true to the old !

XIX.

Yet perhaps in ages
Which thy song-pages
Now dream not of, blue glances or brown
May flash above thee,
Wound thee, or love thee,
More than the looks which pain thee or crown
In soft white girlhood,
Jewel-hood, pearl-hood,—
Smile thee to heaven, or slay with a frown.

XX.

But howso be it
Thou mayest not flee it,
Thy song, thy mission of music and pain :
Pain ; for the poet
Must, heart-wrung, know it,
Or worthless, feeble and false, his strain :
Music ; for these*
Songs blown on the breeze
In the heart of the world as a gift remain.

* Poems, in MS., by Kathleen Gordon, aged fourteen.

GOD AND BEAUTY.

What is the meaning of it all?
  Surely God did not create
  Souls of His people in hate,
  Handing to instruments of fate,
Binding in bitterness of thrall,
His children; giving us gall,

Gall to eat, vinegar to drink;
  We who long for the eyes
  Of Beauty, and look to the prize
  That in arms of endurance lies,
Neither from fires do we shrink;
Heart of not one of us flies.

If God is strong to succeed,
  Then we can trust and abide,
  Rest in the shadow of His side,
  Trust in the God we have tried,
Careless, ready to bleed;
If He is strong to succeed.

Nothing we care for but this,
  That in harmony God shall bring
  Out of each of us some good thing,
  Tuning our voices to sing;
Beauty is one thing and bliss;
Nothing we care for but this.

Why did He give to us love,
  Only to take it away?
  Love the light of a day,
  That lasts but the spring of a spray
Beneath the feet of a dove;
Why did He give to us love?

Love we have seen, and we know,
  Yea, we know she is fair;
  Yea, we have woven her hair
  In our hands, and who shall compare
To her limbs the new-fallen snow?
Love we have seen, and we know.

God we know not, neither see;
  Neither in heaven, nor on earth;
  News was there once of His birth,
  Men shook hands in their mirth,
Women laughed in their glee;
Where now, tell us, is He?

One thing we know, we are sad;
  Yet the face we have seen
  Of Beauty, and hands of our Queen,
  And light of her eyes between
Dark clouds and mists we have had,
And sight of her garments' sheen.

If God loves her as we,
  And with His power (as they say,
  Strong as the might of the day)
  Brings her to pass as we pray,
Souls of us calm can be;
If so He loves her as we.

We who love but the scent
  Of the wave of her hair in the way
  As the flowers the dawn of the day,
  Love her more than our words can say,
And towards the road that she went
Would fall on our knees and pray.

We who have given up all
  To be unto her as the dew
  To the sun; who have sworn to be true;.
  We who are glad in the blue,
But beneath the grey skies fall
As a song-bird struck right through.

If God cares for her face
  Then we love Him, and stand
  Ready to cling to His hand,
  To be led of Him up to the land
Of promise, His own fair place,
A gladsome, a wished-for strand.

If God cares for her not,
  Neither is willing to bring
  Beauty in everything
  To be, let pale priests sing!
Faces with tears we blot,
Fingers of wailing we wring.

But one hope yet avails;
  That out of the smoke and the dust
  Blossom a rose-tree must;
  This is the sole strong trust
To close up a mouth that rails;
This one hope yet avails.

Hope that if we are cast down,
  All unable to stand,
  If our faces are fanned
  By fires of hell, and the land
Is dark, yet God's is the crown
And mighty His strong right hand.

Yea, if He treads upon us,
  Beautiful souls to make,
  Let us not tremble nor quake,
  Let us not quaver nor shake;
Little let God heed us,
If Beauty our Queen is at stake!

She whom of all we adore;
  Loving the feathers of her wings,
  Breath of the air where she sings,
  Sound of the motion she brings
As she shakes the ethereal floor,
And the light that about her clings.

Loving the light of her eyes
  As the bird the breath of the morn,
  As the hound the lilt of the horn,
  As the sun the beauty of dawn,
The face of his bride in the skies
By the mists of night from him torn.

As the sailors watching at night
  The first faint flush in the air
  Of the streaks of the wind-waved hair
  Of Aurora, and fingering fair
Of the clouds touching in fresh light,
As a sign to us all she is there.

As a man tired-out through the day
  The first fresh fall of the dews
  That give to a worker the news
  That at last he may cast off the shoes
Of fatigue, and hasten away,
Nor longer his rest refuse.

As a lover who has not seen
  For a weary sighing of years,
  For a long outpouring of tears,
  For a manifold mist of fears,
The face of a maiden, a queen,
Is glad, when her footstep nears.

As a mother, who longs for her son
  Gone to the fire of the wars,
  Gone as it were to the stars
  So the distance seems, that mars
His features, is like to run
To the sound of home-coming cars.

As all these love, we too
  Are in love with the face of our Queen,
  We poets ; we who have seen
  Her glory, the light of the sheen
Of her raiment ; only a few
In the print of her passing have been.

                                    1870.

SONNET.

THE REVELATIONS OF THE AGES.

Strip off dead husks, the fruit will be the sweeter;
   Shake out dead petals, brighter blooms the
     rose;
Cast off the worn-out shoes, the feet are fleeter,
   Fitter to race along the road that goes,
With many windings, toiling through the ages,
   Revealing ever newer points of view,
Each turn unfolding fresh sweet landscape-pages,
   And broad descents, and hills and valleys new;
Places of which our fathers never dreamed,
   Strange, perilous, by feet of man untrod,
And which to them impassable would have
     seemed,—
   But which we have to traverse, trusting God,
God who for certain leaves no single age
Without its fitting revelation-page.

1870.

TO SHELLEY.

I.

Thy spirit which trod,
Gold-sandalled, a god,
The grass, that blossomed beneath its tread,
At Oxford and saw,
Unsmitten of awe,
The centuries gathered behind it in red
Vast sunset-waves,
Doth it live yet, and saves
Immortal its glory among the dead?

II.

The surf of the sea
Of thought was to thee
But calm clear ripples of inland lakes
Wherein to delight
With free-swimming might
'Mid the blue dear surges and white foam-flakes :
In the old grey town
Thou plaitedst thy crown,
Oxford, and threadedst its harsh thought-brakes.

III.

God was to thee
As the voice of the sea,
As the wings of the surges, the plumes of the blast :.
Little indeed
Of the tame pale creed
That broods blood-stricken above the past
Thy soul did reck ;
Without rein, without check,
It followed its own God-yearning vast.

IV.

Marsh-marigolds
Each dense dyke holds
By Oxford, and long grass-fields at night
Gleam weird and strange,
And the low hill-range
Is purple at sunset against the bright
Sky orange or red ;
And the moonrays wed
O'er the silvery river the last faint light.

V.

These thou didst see,
And seen too of me
Were the weird grey hollows, the wild long hills,
The gleaming expanse
Of the ripples that dance
On Isis, and all that the swift gaze fills
From Iffley to where
The white waves tear
At Sandford the foam that the fierce stream spills.

VI.

Then thou didst fly
The dim mist-sky
Of England and sangest in Italy's vales,
More sweet than the sound
Heard there without bound
As it throbs and rises, ascends and fails,
Of the nightingale-song
When its ecstasy strong
Now triumphs and leaps, now weeps and wails.

VII.

What didst thou know
Of love ?   Was it woe,
Or gladness passing the frail mute dream
Of men who aspire
But find not a lyre
Like thine, so watch but thy gold harp-gleam
As it glittereth swept
By the fingers that slept,
That rested, never from song's bright theme ?

VIII.

Oh, love to thee
Was as soft as the sea
At softest even : it was not the sound
Of the fierce-tongued surges
The fierce breeze scourges—
It was as the blossoms that star the ground,
Filled with perfume
And glory of bloom,
A mantle of beauty to plain and mound.

IX.

Were the women who wove
For thee raiment of love
As stars of passion within thine hair?
Bright stars merely,
Or loved more nearly—
Who was thy bride, most sweet of the fair
Women who gave
Lips gracious to save,
And filled thy summer with rose-sweet air?

X.

What laughter of bright
Lips, beauty of white
Limbs ever sufficed for, satisfied thee?
What rose was as red
As thy dreams on it shed?
Yea, thy thoughts were more white than the waves
of the sea,
And the heavens unclear
By thy song-sky dear,
Wherethrough thou wast wont to exult and flee.

XI.

What rich buds even
In Italy's heaven
Were rich as the buds in the dreams of thy song?
What marvellous flow
Of ripples aglow
Danced gold in the sunlight, white in the throng
Of the white moonbeams,
Through the winged soft dreams
Of thy spirit alert, divine and strong?

XII.

Oh, blossoms indeed,
A princely meed,
Thou hast given us, Shelley : and skies and seas,
And the voice of a rhyme
Unending, sublime,   •
And the laughter of fays in the leafage of trees,
And the tidal motion
Of song's sweet ocean,
The glitter of insects, the humming of bees.

XIII.

The universe
In thy pure verse
Gloweth and floweth, speaketh and sings :
From rose to lily,
From vale to hilly
Far rock-bound region on far-spread wings
Thou floatest and seizest
What bloom thou pleasest ;
Yea, what thou willest, thy quick harp brings.

XIV.

And so in the sphere
Of high thought, clear
And brave thy voice is, fearless, unchained :
Thou wast not afraid
Of Calvary's shade ;
Free on the hill-top thy foot remained :
Thou wast not bound
By the calm sweet sound
Of Christ's voice, nor by the Church-crimes stained.

XV.

Pure of the flood
Of innocent blood
Spilt by the Church thou wast : for a friend
Christ thou knewest
And in skies bluest
Of great thought soughtest him, didst not bend ;
Thy bright head never
Need bend, nor ever
Can Christ in the sheer song-land contend.

XVI.

He hath his crown,
And thou thine own,
Shelley,—thy song-crown perfect indeed :
His wreath of pain
He hath, and his fane,
And the thorns that yet on the white brow bleed ;
But thou, an immortal,
By thine own portal
Mayest enter the gates of the God we need.

XVII.

For England in song
Untrammelled and strong
Yearn we to hear now, not to be told
Of deeds outworn,
In a far land born ;
We need but love, to our hearts to hold,
And the lips of the rose
That in England blows,
Woman, sweeter than women of old.

XVIII.

Not Palestine,
Nor the fig and the vine,
But the corn and the clover, the clear-eyed maid
On the cliff-top standing
With glance commanding
Searching our broad seas,—the oak-trees' shade,
The purple heather,
' The grey wild weather
In England, the furze-crowned fern-lined glade.

XIX.

This we need :
Thou gavest a creed,
Shelley, which brings us high help now ;
God in the soul
Of each, and the whole
Of the leafy wide world, not one bough
Of a palm-tree faded,
And grasped in jaded
Priest's hands—broken and tangled how !

XX.

Thou wast the first
Through whose song burst
The chant of England, freeing her soul
From the dry harsh letter,
The ruinous fetter
Of creeds that around her white limbs stole
As ravening snakes
In the dead-branch brakes :
She gives thee her rose-heart, gives thee the whole ?

TO KEATS.

I.

O crowned immortal
Who through the portal
Of life didst pass to a deathless tomb,
Where art thou singing
And thine hands bringing
Immortals blossoms of grander bloom
Than those that awoke
At thy swift harp-stroke
Ere our earth failed thee and rang thy doom ?

II.

What dreams surrounded
Thy young soul bounded
And barred on all sides as thou didst sing,
Of cowslip and daisy
And spring morns hazy,
Soft-brooding ever with young white wing
Above our meadows,
And through time's shadows
Moving, a song-god, an uncrowned king ?

III.

What dreams we know not,
Which thy songs show not,
Filled thy young spirit and smote thine heart
With stroke as of oars
Nigh musical shores,
Some with sweet pleasure and some with smart?
What thoughts supreme
In a flash, in a dream,
Of love, of life, of thine own fair Art?

IV.

Ne'er wast thou wingless,
But alway stingless,
Pure alway, gentle and tender and high:
A poet indeed
With thine heart for a creed
And thy temple the uttermost deep blue sky,
And the sound of the sea
For hymnal to thee,
And the voice of the breeze for thy soul's own sigh.

V.

The stars were thine own
And thy locks were blown
By the wind of the night as a spirit indeed
Of friendliest greeting;
Thy heart swift-beating
Went traversing valley and dingle and mead,
Finding in each
Songs sweeter than speech
Of the birds who sang to thee, tuned thy reed.

VI.

Greek-souled, Greek-eyed,
Thy spirit espied
'Things hidden from all of us, given to thee
For balm and delight;
Full oft through the night
'Or the tangle of leaves 'mid the boughs of a tree
Came nymphs new-risen
For thee from their prison,
And mermaids shone in the gulfs of the sea.

VII.

The dead ideal
To thee was real;
And real life gave thee one strange sweet dream:
Thou diedst crying
On one, far-flying
In spirit to where our white waves gleam
From Italy's shore;
One loved as of yore,
And sought while launched upon death's still
stream.

VIII.

What hast thou now,
Keats? visited how
Is the heaven-high spirit by love's glance bright?
What tresses are fair
In the summer-soft air,
More summer-soft ever for pulse of the flight
Of song-woven pinions
Which flood the dominions
Of death with torrents of golden light?

IX.

Hath thy kiss lighted
Soft and invited
On dear lips redder than lips of queens
Who make this earth to us
Gracious in mirth, to us
Bringing the glory of all sweet scenes ?
Whom hast thou wedded,
White-souled, gold-headed ?
What breast above thee with rapture leans ?

X.

Oh, are they fairer,
Those queens, and rarer
In passionate beauty than flowers below
Loved and proclaimed of us ?
Are they ashamed of us ?
Seek they for singers whose lips they know
In heaven, and we hear not,
Worship, revere not,—
Scorn they the passions our songs bestow ?

XI.

Hath love the splendour,
The dear glow tender,
In heaven that crowns us toiling and tired ?
Hast thou Keats fashioned
New lyrics impassioned,
By love of celestial sweet eyes fired ?
Now is thy song
As soft and more strong,
By the women of deathland sought and inspired ?

XII.

Oh are they sweet
With lily-clear feet,
And lips like the scent of the first May rose
In a shower at morn;
And their laugh is it born
In the high pure air where no frail foot goes,
But only the singer's
Firm step that lingers
·Gentian-like 'mid the untouched snows ?

XIII. ·

Thy dreams now are blessed,
Thy soul is at rest
Having passed from the earth where never a bard
Hath trodden save sadly,
Endlessly, madly,
To struggle in fate's steel bondage hard,
Till sweet death came
And her plumage of flame
Left the prison-barriers crushed and charred.

XIV.

Then comes the sky,
The night wind's sigh,
The sense of release and the leaves of the trees
Tenderly dancing
And gold stars glancing
O'er billows of limitless fetterless seas,
And the terrible gladness,
Transfiguring sadness,
Of visions of moonlit and measureless leas.

XV.

One day to each of us,
Close, within reach of us,
Comes the waft of the rose-like breath
Of the passionate bride
For whom we have sighed,
Yea, the passionate exquisite bosom of death,
And the lips of the night
Soft, flower-light,
And the word that the night's mouth whispering
saith.

XVI.

Then shall we see
The kingdom of thee,
Keats? all thy treasure uncounted, untold?
Thy brides in the sky
And thine ecstasy high,
And thy laughter as tender and clear as of old,
And thy singing supreme,
Like love's through a dream,
Rich from thy god's mouth moulded of gold.

XVII.

Or hast thou found
And conquered and bound
Some sweet flower-singer as soft and as young
In heaven, and chained her,
Loved and retained her
For ever while ever thy glad lips sung
Perfect, divine to her,
Sweet line by line to her—
Wonderful honeyed decoys of thy tongue?

XVIII.

Oh, is she listening,
The soft eyes glistening
At all the magic of thy fond strain ?
Now no more lonely
Thou art but only
Alone with one in the love-god's fane :
Rested at last
With sorrow in the past
Dead, while the flowers of the past remain.

XIX.

Through the soft June light,
Summer clear moonlight,
Conquering spirits, I cry to your land :
Crown us at last too,
Suffering the blast too
Of sorrow; stretch down a white strong hand
To singers who need
Your presence indeed,
Who yet uncrowned on the dim earth stand.

XX.

O bride of Keats
Whose heart now beats
For the singer whose spirit knows pain no more,
Remember that we
'Mid the waves of the sea
Of time yet struggle,—hear thou the roar
Of the breakers : oh aid
Till we too have made
The ultimate haven, the sorrowless shore !

THREE SONNETS.

I.

THE CHRISTS OF THE AGES.

There are whose spirit-pangs do far exceed
  The pangs the Hebrew weaveth in his crown :
  Not on one Son of God high God smiled down,
But such throughout the foolish centuries bleed.
Oh, thrice accursed is the small dim creed
  That cramps its votaries' souls before one
      Cross ;
  Poor mole-eyed spirits ! they count all suffer-
    ings dross
Save Christ's,—the English blood-rose but a
    weed !

The Christs o' the ages, men and women fair
  In spirit as was Christ, or fairer far,
Are crucified indeed—no perfumed air
  Of incense-worship crowns them, and no star
Gleams apostolic, fiery, o'er their head :
Men worship not; God worships them instead.

    (*Written on the eve of Good Friday, March 25, 1880.*)

II.

THE CRUCIFIXION OF MANHOOD.

(For Good Friday, 1880.)

To-day, as ever, pale mankind is nailed
 Upon the bitter cross ; the people go
 To weep false tears o'er overrated woe,—
Weeping because one far-off fair life failed.
And what of heights of manhood left unscaled
 To-day, because this piteous farce runs so ?
 What of the sufferers dying beneath snow
Of want of love to-day, by no hymns hailed ?

Ah ! shall there be an Easter morn for these,
 As through the blood-stained centuries not one
  day
 Hath not loomed like Good Friday gaunt and
  grey
Upon them ; from grim immemorial seas
 Of timeless suffering, grievous, marred and
  wan,
 What Easter torch shall light the spirit of
  man ?

III.

THE CRUCIFIXION OF WOMANHOOD.

And what of woman? Shall she not arise
   Splendid as risen Christ on Easter morn,—
   Seeking, dew-kissed, sun-crowned, a flower
     new-born,
Untraversed haunts of unfamiliar skies?
Shall not the sweet God shine within her eyes?
   Shall not her swordless white hand laugh to
     scorn
   The pale black-armoured foes who would have
     torn
Her banner down, that floated lily-wise?

Oh, Christ is risen; leave his grave in peace.
   Rise thou, O woman, from thine own poor
     dreams;
   Lo! even for thee an Easter morning gleams
Triumphant, and thine utter woes shall cease
   Mayhap: no more shall flow the sacred blood
   Of crucified, sad, tortured womanhood.

(Written on Easter Eve, March 27, 1880.)

TO WOMAN.

I.

Not of any wonder
High in heaven clear,
Soaring beyond thunder,
Making for man's ear
Music that falls divinely through the azure sheer.

II.

Not of any skylark
High in heaven I sing :
Loftier than the high lark
With my songful wing
I would sail, glad-seeking yet a fairer thing.

III.

Fairer thing, and sweeter
Than the lark at dawn ;
Tenderer, completer,
Out of God's heart gone ;
More silver-voiced than birds, swift-footed as a
fawn.

IV.

Glorious in the azure,
White above the sea,
Man's supremest pleasure,
Grand in purity,
Woman thou art: and heaven I find, in seeking thee.

V.

Wonderful thy song is,
  Fairer than the lark ;
Tender it and strong is,
  Bursting through the dark,
Till all the heavens for wonder hush themselves
  and hark.

VI.

Marvellous thy singing ;
  Sweet thy snow-white form,
Ever to man's clinging,
  Faithful through each storm,
Every surge of anguish, tender still and warm.

VII.

Through the night of trouble,
  Through thy long sad past,
Thou hast sung; now double,
  Sweet, thy song at last ;
Sing, for thy night is over, thine enemies down-
  cast.

VIII.

Sing in the glad clear morning,
  O woman-spirit,—sing :
Thy life-long sorrows scorning ;
  Soft-brushing with white wing
Aside each hindering hostile pestilential thing.

IX.

Bring to man the gladness
 That he fain would know;
Banish all our sadness;
 Make an end of woe;
Create a perfect heaven amid thy bowers below.

X.

Sweet, create God's heaven,
 Golden, glad, and clear,
In earth's valleys even;
 Yea, love, even here:
Bring the divine redemption with thy presence
near.

XI.

Be to man a saviour
 Gentle-souled and white,
Sweet in pure behaviour,
 Glad in modest might;
Assert thy woman's sceptre, claim thy queenly
right.

XII.

Be to earth a blossom
 Soft, divine indeed;
Take man to thy bosom,
 Man, in utmost need;
Give to his endless yearning, gentle lady, heed.

XIII.

Build thy bower of roses,
    Golden, sweet, divine
On earth : where love reposes
    'Neath ivy and woodbine
Build thou thy palace, made imperishably thine.

XIV.

Let thy wondrous singing
    Sound o'er earthly seas ;
Lo ! thy voice is ringing
    Silver in each breeze
Of summer, and amid the green thick-foliaged
    trees.

XV.

God in thee revealing
    All his tender grace
Shines ; his love is stealing,
    Love, throughout thy face ;
Thine hand upon earth's meadows, blossoms in
    each place.

XVI.

Where thou art, the lily
    Straightway doth appear ;
Roses o'er the hilly
    Rocky fields and sheer
Bloom ; thou bringest eternal glory, sweetheart,
    here.

XVII.

All my song I render,
Lady, unto thee;
Worshipping thy splendour,
All thy purity:
Listening to thy low laughter and thy magic glee.

XVIII.

All the bending glory
Of the golden corn,
Crests of billows hoary,
Crimson clouds at morn,—
And all earth's countless splendours, for thy sake
are born.

XIX.

Not, like Shelley's wonder,
Singing in the sky,
Not sad thoughts from yonder
Bringest thou, sweet, nigh;
But only utter gladness laughing in thine eye.

XX.

Only utter gladness
Sounding in thy voice,
Now thy former sadness
Letteth thee rejoice,
Having fled back for ever, like a tempest-noise.

XXI.

Bring us sweet redemption,
    Sweet one, in thy breast;
Virtue, and exemption
    From the weary quest
For what might be more fitting, what the eternal
    best.

XXII.

Thou the eternal best art,
    Thou the endless queen,
Thou man's perfect rest art,
    Tender, white, serene,
The sweetest of all songsters that have ever been.

XXIII.

Sweetest of all singers,
    Softest of all birds,
Flowers within thy fingers,
    Laughter in thy words,
Lo! for thy service now his sword man's spirit
    girds.

XXIV.

Not an angel—fairer;
    Lovelier, thou art:
Not a skylark—rarer;
    Gifted with a heart
Even more full of songs that down the deep blue
    dart.

XXV.

All my heart and fire
 Unto thee I bring;
Bless thou, love, my lyre, .
 Let it nobly sing
Thee the eternal queen of every poet-king.

XXVI.

All my yearning spirit,
 Love, to-night I raise;
Let my soul inherit
 At the end of days
That heaven whence thou stoopest, coveting our
 lays.

XXVII.

For our lays thou lovest,
 Though thou art a queen,
Woman; though thou movest
 Over floors serene,
Golden in skies untroubled, measureless in sheen.

XXVIII.

Yea, our songs thou hearest,
 And thou dost bestow
Power; yea, love, thou carest
 For thy bards below
Snatching at sacred joys they may not fully know.

K

XXIX.

O thou rose eternal,
    Heavenly love, made fair
Not as flowers diurnal,
    Filling all the air
Of utter heaven with fragrance passing man's
    speech rare ;

XXX.

Take this song and bear it
    Through the clouds of night;
For thy garland wear it,
    Smile with smile most bright
Upon my soul, and make it, as thy soul is, white!

———

TO THE ENGLISH POETS OF THE PAST.

Ye whose lips were wet
    With the self-same sea,
    Hearken unto me:
Let now my voice by your victorious harps be met.

Ye too struggled on;
    Following after fame
    Till at length it came—
But came not till your mortal shapes were dead
    and gone.

Ye too loved and spake
    In the English air:
    Found the same flowers fair;
Marked the same tides upon the same white cliff-
    sides break.

Ye too in your time
    Knew love's wonder here:
    Found love's message dear;
Recorded love's worth in imperishable rhyme.

Oh that in the end
    I may join, I too,
    You great voice,—and you,—
May touch the hands of many a true bay-wreathèd
    friend!

Surely with the same
　　Passion of pure love
　　Which your hearts did move,
I too love the shores wherein ye won your fame.

Singing in an age
　　When the noises sharp
　　Drown out many a harp,
Imperious battle harder than your war we wage.

Yea, if but one heart
　　Doth respond to ours,
　　Resting in our bowers
Of song, it is reward thought great for living Art.

Yea, if but one hears ;
　　And if dead we find
　　All the bards who twined
Round their brows of old the laurels of past
　years—

If but these we find
　　Gladdened by our song,
　　All our souls are strong
To face the bitter days of obloquy unkind.

For the self-same land
　　Shall receive our word,
　　Over which was poured
The sacred stream of song from many a former
　hand.

And though in our day
Listeners are but few,
Splendider is too
The victory of the voice which nothing can gain-
say.

The victory of the harp
Sure-voiced as the sea:
O'er which there can be
No mist nor vapour flung by foolish tongues that
carp.

O great English bards
Grant us in the end
Triumph, and extend
To each who struggleth now 'mid waves whose
force retards,

As each soul deserves,
Greeting from on high,
Help, and victory;
If but to the utter end each battles on, nor
swerves.

SO HE CEASED TO BELIEVE IN MAN.

A thinker, young, was worried and stung
  By gibes of friends and priests;
The peace he sought could not be brought
  By pleasure or jovial feasts;
A peace they proffered, a rest they offered
      Far from the battle's van—
      So he ceased to believe in Man!

He ceased to believe in Man and receive
  The gifts Man has to hold:
The strong despair whose face is fair,
  Yea, sweeter than wrought gold;
The endless scope of desperate hope;
      The proud Church waved her fan—
      So he ceased to believe in Man!

He could no more upon the shore
  Delight in ocean's waves;
He could no longer stand far stronger
  Than foam-white leagues of graves;
His power was spent, his head was bent,
      He trembled, pale and wan—
      So he ceased to believe in Man!

The glorious earth no more with mirth
  Unutterable delayed him :
The pleasant flowers and woodbine bowers
  Had all, he thought, betrayed him ;
The roses red were fickle and dead ;
      He could not life's girth span—
      So he ceased to believe in Man !

The wondrous sound of music bound
  His being now in vain ;
A woman's eyes (wherein there lies
  A cure for every pain)
Could not entreat, were no more sweet ;
      He failed their depth to scan—
      So he ceased to believe in Man !

And heaven-sent love was but a dove,
  No lustre on its pinions ;
The struggle of thought went all for nought,
  The woods were death's dominions ;
The azure sky was hollow and dry,
      Earth groaned beneath a ban—
      So he ceased to believe in Man !

SO HE ENTERED THE CHURCH OF ROME.

Then pale priests came with comfort tame
  But grateful to his soul;
They offered him a temple dim,
  They brought an honeyed bowl;
He could not shrink, he chose to drink;
    He sought a quiet home—
    So he entered the Church of Rome!

He ceased to plead, he ceased to bleed,
  He cannot struggle now;
He cannot fight, he has lost the light,
  It flames not on his brow;
Far from the rattle of earth's wild battle
    His frail feet longed to roam—
    So he entered the Church of Rome!

He longed for peace and calm release
  From all the labour of thought;
He longed for pleasure and gentle leisure—
  He has found the gifts he sought:
High thought is curbed, he is not disturbed;
    He yearned for a painted dome—
    So he entered the Church of Rome!

His heaven is sure, his bliss secure,
    The angels wait for him ;
His harp is ready beyond the eddy
    Of death's stream cold and dim ;
His bright robe waits beyond the gates
        Of heaven : he shunned life's foam—
        So he entered the Church of Rome !

His joy is certain : he draws the curtain
    On earth, and its windy fate ;
He cares not now what furrows plough
    Our foreheads, what sore weight
Of trouble and care we have to bear ;
        His feet stuck in earth's loam—
        So he entered the Church of Rome !

He shrank from thought—the terror it brought,
    Its passionate joy as well :
He shall not see the life of the free,
    His high Church is his hell ;
He shall not enter the fair centre
        Of Man's perfect home,
        Far from the Church of Rome.

CHRIST AND WOMAN.

Are there not, O king,
　　King of many lands,
Brooding with broad wing
　　Over seas and sands,
　　Free yet from thine hands,
Full many shores whereto free joyous spirits cling?

Are there not, O lord
　　Of the church-fed air
Which is round us poured
　　For our birth-day fare
　　In England everywhere,
Yet souls untrammelled girt with courage for a
　　sword?

If our women find
　　In thee all they seek,
Deaf and pale and blind,
　　Noble not but weak—
　　Yet hath not some cheek
Of woman flushed for love of her own kith and
　　kind?

If our churches groan
   With the praise they pour
In their weary tone
   On thee evermore,
   Yet hath not some shore
Crowns of another Christ, and other worship
   known ?

   Is the rose more red
      Since the Saviour's birth ?
   Or the lily's head
      Tenderer in worth ?
      Greener is the earth ?
Doth any Lazarus here come smiling from the
   dead ?

   Do the loaves increase
      For *our* needy crowd ?
   Do our terrors cease ?
      Doth the ghostlike shroud
      Of sorrow at the loud
Mandate of any Christ divide, disclosing peace ?

   Have the high sheer waves
      At Christ's bidding spared
   Seamen,—have the graves
      That their gulfs prepared
      Yielded souls that dared
To tempt the awful deep back from their frothy
   caves ?

Have the breakers stood
　　Silent at the touch
Of a Saviour good,
　　Rescuing from their clutch
　　Souls he valued much?
Have blossoms burned new-born on rods of barren
　　wood?

Hath the grave again
　　Opened to set free
Any sons of men,—
　　Given to liberty
　　Any soul that we
Have marked its iron bars and bitter paling pen?

What hath Christ for these
　　English yearning souls
Done that they should cease,
　　As the world-wave rolls
　　Onward over shoals
And sunken reefs, to seek in their own spirits
　　peace?

Peace within the shores
　　Where their life was born,
Over which God pours
　　Crimson blush of morn,
　　Which he clothes with corn,—
Round which their sails are white, and round
　　which throb their oars.

Pleasure in the land
 That indeed their own
They may call, and stand
 On it as a throne,
 By its breezes blown,
Girt with its cliffs and yellow wastes of sea-
 washed sand.

Oh, is this not ours,
 All this island-shore?
Green and glad with bowers;
 Undismayed by war;
 Over which there pour
Fresh from God's fruitful hand the ever-fruitful
 showers.

Is it not thine own,
 Brother? why then seek
Alien shores and groan,
 Awe-struck at the peak
 Of Sinai, or some creek
Whose rocky bluffs once rang to Christ's alluring
 tone?

Why this discontent?
 Why this wild desire,
Longing ever bent
 With increasing fire
 On an Eastern lyre,
That wayward and harsh-toned uncertain instru-
 ment?

Are not the strong seas
   Of our pent-up coast
Touched by wintry breeze
   Music deep ? a host
   Of singers we may boast,
Yea may not we ?—the birds among our summer
   trees ?

And have not we the grace
   Of perfect womanhood
Among us—yea, each face,
   Sweet and pure and good,
   Womanly in mood,
Brings God before us, God made plain in every
   place.

Christs we have, and kings :
   Women-Christs divine,
Bearing snowier wings
   Than the wings that shine,
   Noble in outline,
Upon the Christ who on the rain-dyed gibbet
   swings.

Is not Woman more
   Even than the rose ?
Shall she not, too, soar
   Past all earthly woes,
   Till bright gates disclose
In heaven heroic hearts for her too to adore ?

Are not her lips sweet,
And her tresses fair?
And shall she retreat,
Hustled through the air,
When her foes declare
That God's step sounds alone in Christ's ap-
proaching feet?

Is not every bride
Unto us as pure
As the Christ who sighed
In the groves obscure
Where e'en now endure
Stories that drip with blood, memories of how he
died?

Did he rise alone?
Shall not we too rise
To our fitting throne,
Triumph in our eyes,
Cleaving sundered skies,—
Have we not too the Father, and his glory
known?

Hath the Father one
Only child and heir?
Favourite chief son,
Who alone may share
All the treasures fair
Amassed since first his Sire creative toil begun?

Shall not Woman rise
        Bursting all the bars
That now mock her sighs,
        Sweep along the stars—
        All that stays and mars
Long left behind in lower undertrodden skies?

Shall she not surpass
        Saviours and ascend
To the seas of glass,
        All high heaven for friend?
        Is there any end
To blossoms that smile upward, round her, from
    the grass?

Hath the Holy Ghost
        Not a cliff-top lair
Somewhere in our coast?
        Is not English air
        Sweet enough and fair
Enough to bring down many a bright angelic
    host?

White and pure indeed
        Are the angels seen
With us, whose feet bleed
        'Mid the grasses green;
        Thick clouds fail to screen
From us high heaven; we have the angel-help we
    need.

Not in this our age
  Did the Christ-king rise :
Not his war we wage
  'Neath our stormier skies,
  Echo not his sighs;
Contend not, as did he, with winds' and waters'
  rage.

Rather in the stress
  Of our surging thought
Struggle we no less :
  No less hearts have brought
  Purified of aught
That might obscure or cloud the faith our tongues
  confess.

The utter faith in man
  And the Power that leads
Onward through life's span
  Man,—who toils and bleeds,
  Suffers and succeeds,
Completes at last the work his birthday breath
  began.

Faith in the great soul
  Human, and the Power
Latent in the whole,
  Sweet in the rose-bower,
  Tender in love's hour,
Who, silent, works on towards the foreseen cer-
  tain goal.

L

Faith in man's soul's light,
    And the perfect doom
Of day to follow night;
    Night again with gloom
    To rest us, and entomb
The sadness of the day, healing with gentle might.

Faith in the course of things,
    Certain and sublime,
Towards the utmost springs
    Of morning : towards a clime
    Sunnier, and a rhyme
Beating more gladsome yet through broad crea-
    tion's wings.

Therefore not one King
    Worship we, but crown
Man, and 'neath man's wing
    Gladly rest,—and down
    Towards life's furrows brown
We look; no more our hands round heaven's
    flower-stalks cling.

Woman we elect
    Tender snow-white queen :
Man, the lord, is decked
    Now in lordly sheen;
    Priests who came between
Man and the Power that made, with anger we
    reject.

For God's mouth shall bend,
Tender, unto each,
Kissing each as Friend,
If we will but reach
Upward, and beseech,
Fearless, the Power that wrought, to mould us to
the end.

TO APOLLO.

I.

O King Apollo
O'er mount and hollow
Do I not follow with weary feet?
Do I, pursuer,
Where skies are bluer
And meadows softer, recede, retreat?
Thy gold hair flaming
In front flight shaming
Leads onward ever, than stars more sweet.

II.

How many follow
Thee, lord Apollo,
Yet lay no hands on thy garments' hem!
They sink down weary
By road-side dreary,
Sink, and the world hears nought of them:
Their harps are taken,
Their god forsaken,
And the austere lips of the god condemn.

III.

O condemnation
From heaven-high station
Severely spoken,—O gold-haired king!
Let me swerve never
But, patient ever,
At thy feet or in thy pathway sing :
Sing by the meadows,
And through the shadows,
Soft-brushing grasses with ghost-like wing.

IV.

By river flowing,
By white tide glowing
Of ocean's margent, by mead and rill;
By star-lit valleys
Whence thy foot sallies
O sudden song-god and all is still;
By dawn, by daylight,
By gold star-ray-light,
By sweet moon-beam-light; 'neath shade of hill :

V.

'Mid grass, 'mid clover,
Swift-foot, a rover,
'Mid golden ranks of the gold-haired corn—
Gold-haired as thou
Of the snow-white brow
Whence all the music of earth was born—
Through darkness deep
When frail souls sleep,
At murky midnight, at crimson morn :

VI.

Through youth, through seasons
When love's swift treasons
Are surging round us like waves of seas;
Through manhood's stiller
Strong years O filler
Of all the air with the song of the breeze—
Through life to death
Let thy sweet song-breath
Lift me and waft me whither it please!

VII.

I dread not sorrow
If by it I borrow
A strength more ample, a lyre more true;
If by the pain-wave,
The red blood-rain-wave,
My wings more potent, invade the blue
Of loftier heaven;
Then would I even
'Mid pangs my tremulous song renew.

VIII.

But surely, surely,
Patiently, purely,
I *have* thee followed, O lord, O king!
I have not trembled,
Nor quaked, dissembled
Before the world,—but the deep pure thing
Thou gavest me, loudly,
Strongly and proudly,
I have not ceased, through life, to sing.

IX.

I have not lost it,
Nor blurred nor crossed it
With threads invasive of mere self-will;
My message clearly
Have spoken—nearly
The sole night-singer when all was still
In the hushed dark sometimes;
Till there would come times
When all thy woods loud lyres would fill.

X.

The gift thou gavest
Among the bravest,
The dearest, sweetest, of loves and friends,
I've used; not heeding
Feet full-oft bleeding
And heart that the world's sharp spear-head rends:
Now may I rest
On the night's dim breast
As at thy coming my pale chant ends.

XI.

Lo! thou appearest
Apollo and clearest
The heaven above thee with awful might:
The clouds before thee
Retreat—high o'er thee
Within thy tresses the sun flames bright:
And the seas thy footing
Follow with floating
Ripples of august golden light.

XII.

Now let me, weary,
　The black night dreary
Evade for ever, now thou art here :
　My song is ended
　Now, fierce, extended
Across the skies thy white steeds rear !
　My song is over
　Now thou, song's lover,
As gold-haired bridegroom dost appear.

XIII.

Take my pale singing :
　Let some notes ringing
High upward, skyward, remain, abide :
　But oh thy laughter
　So sweet, comes after,
So silver-clear o'er the charmed sea-tide ;
　And what can singers
　Of earth with fingers
Feeble fashion for song thy bride ?

XIV.

Is she too golden
　Of locks, and holden
Within her hands is a harp-stem true?
　Or black-haired rather,
　Nereus her father,
Did she step forth from the sea-caves blue
　With musical feet
　Apollo to meet,—
With grey glance subtle, snow-white of hue ? .

XV.

Yea, she was gracious
Within the spacious
Deep domes of singing beneath the waves;
And what can our song,
Our pale earth's flower-song
That twines with roses the grass of graves
Be to the tender
And soft-voiced splendour
Of white seas breaking in dim sea-caves?

XVI.

Yet hear our flower-song,
Our red-rose-bower song,
And take it tenderly, great song-king;
For there are in it
Not chirp of linnet
And song-thrush only, but notes that ring
Forth sweeter, greater
Than these O hater
Of all things little, O gold of wing!

XVII.

Not songs that languish
But deep heart-anguish
And throbs unspoken of nights and days,
These, these, we bring thee
And with them ring thee,
Not with the flower-stalks, not with the bays:
Oh bend Apollo
And hear the hollow
Groan of the earth's voice, take it as praise.

XVIII.

While thou wast wedded,
Our groans have eddied
From lonely bosoms upon the breeze :
While thou wast toying
With thy bride, cloying
Thy soul with sweetness, our soul did freeze,
Pallid and crownless
And naked, renownless,
Hopeless as arms of the storm-lashed trees !

XIX.

Therefore remember
With us December
Abides while summer O gold-haired king
Is with thee alway,
And thy bright hallway
With laughter of red lips laughs and may ring :
Alone not ever
Thou wast,—yea never
With lone lips hadst thou had heart to sing.

XX.

So when thou flamest
In dawn and aimest
Thy final arrows at earth's last night,
Forget not those who
In pain arose,—who
Sang to thee, song-god, when nought was bright
Save only the endless
Love then thought friendless
Wherewith they longed for thee, longed for thy
  light.

Feb. 10, 1880.

TO GERTRUDE ENTERING A
CONVENT.

Ah! weak and frail—but yet so sweet, so pure!
Thou art English, rosebud! yet could'st not endure
The strong salt breeze, but must thy soul secure
   Within these close-barred flowerless scentless
      gates.

Thou art English : yet the sweet and stalwart
   breeze
That laughs delighted 'mid our bright oak trees
And sweeps across the emerald lavish leas
   Thou could'st not bear; what breeze thy coming
      waits ?

O all shut in apart from suns and stars
Within these bloomless barren spouseless bars,
How black a cowardly crime thy girlhood mars,
   Thine English girlhood, spoilt by froward fates !'

How deep a weak-souled crime thy life begins !
How crowned thy forehead is with others' sins !
Oh, if the eternal Bridegroom thee, sweet, wins,
   Thou art not won, if love's pursuit abates !

Yea, if love's English foot throughout the gloom
Thee follows not, nor cares to seek thy tomb,
Thou art lost—yea, lost, for all the hectic bloom
   That heaven upon thy pale cheek reinstates.

Thou art lost, abandoned, sold: thy body young
That English true lips might have loved and sung
Is buried deep, deep; round thy neck have clung
    Foul serpents of the dusk, like hissing hates.

O flower, white flower, why wilt thou thus away?
O rose, sweet rose, why will thy footsteps stray?
Lo! night before thee lies, but crimson day
    Behind; oh pause ere yet the last bolt grates.

O blossom, blossom, wandering down the track,
Alone, uncherished, wilt thou not turn back?
Thou know'st not yet how dark it is alack!
    Within that vault thy purpose meditates.

By every English rose of thee a part
Pause maiden, slaughter not thy young fair heart:
Yea, drop from thy white hand the priest-forged
    dart;
    Lo! rose-like love thy being renovates.

By every English woman glad and strong
Hear thou the swift notes of an English song:
Do not thy white soul this unfathomed wrong:
    Do England's soul no wrong; heed not these
    baits.

The great white soul of England calleth thee:
In every white wave of the thundering sea
Its mandate sounds; it sounds again through me;
    Pause, ere thine hand thine own soul dissipates.

Pause, Gertrude; by thine own dear English name
That burns our hearts with longing like a flame
Do not thy soul and England's soul this shame:
    Pause, ere thy fall our foemen's craving sates.

A WHITE ROSE IN NOVEMBER.

I thought it was summer when I saw the white
    rose !
Oh can it be November, when so bright a blossom
    glows ?
The tender blossom-maiden I place within my
    song,
To bloom therein, and smile therein, the whole
    year long !

It cannot be November, it must be tender June :
The birds amid the tree-tops will wake and whisper
    soon :
The seas, blue-bright for summer, will chant their
    chorus strong
And flowers will crown our foreheads, the glad
    year long !

Oh summer ever reaches us, if but a summer-
    maid,
Sweet June wreathed in her tresses, gold August
    in each braid,
Smiles, laughs; if but her accents, so silver-sweet
    and clear,
Bring all the songs of spring-time, yea, every
    throstle, near.

I knew it was summer when I saw the white
   rose !
Through not another blossom so sweet a beauty
   glows ;
I know not any blossom so tender-sweet and
   white,   •
Though many blossoms richer have flamed upon
   my sight.

It always must be summer when the white rose
   sings,
With music in her outspread sun-seeking petal-
   wings !
It always must be summer where the white rose
   gleams,
For summer's self pursues her and glitters in her
   dreams.

O white rose, white rose, soon you will be far
From England and my singing ; but watch some
   clear glad star
That shineth over England above the Indian sea
And send your love, soft, star-like, by that glad
   star to me.

O white rose, white rose, soon you will be wed,
And all our days of laughter and singing will be
   dead ;
But white rose, white rose, take my kiss away
Hid soft amid your petals, and therein let it stay !

Hid sweet amid your petals; oh therein let it
    rest,
White rose, white rose, as in a scented nest
Of young soft blessed fragrance; and when you
    watch the foam
That breaks o'er Indian sand-banks, wave hands to
    me at home!

                       Nov. 16, 1878.

TO CHRIST.

Have we not garlands in these latter days
Whether of gold or rosebuds or of bays—
   Have we not fitting joys and loves to treasure—
Snow-stars of winter, green light spring-tide
      sprays,
   Passion with heart-throbs tender beyond
      measure ;
Friendship of manhood, woman's love and praise ?

Have we not white seas beating round our shores
And in our ironbound creeks the throb of oars ?
   Have we not all the early summer sweetness
Of morning, and delight that even pours
   Upon us at the burning day's completeness—
And the same sunset's cloud-built golden doors ?

What is there wanting ? Are the skies not gold ?
The clouds not tipped with crimson as of old ?
   Is the gold hair of women grown less ample—
The fire of love a worn-out thing and cold—
   Yea, do the heavy-footed centuries trample
All that humanity would clasp, enfold ?

May we not mark within our own grey sea
Tints fairer than o' the lake of Galilee?
  Is any flower than the English rose more
    splendid?
Are women than our women more divine?
  Are sweeter sprays and goldener extended
In Jewish fields than English lush woodbine?

Can we not meet the high God face to face,
Yea, pant and wrestle for his pure embrace?
  Oh, what have we to do with legends devious
On whose clear brows the English God hath
    shone?
  Why bind our souls by lore of ages previous—
Why guide our spirits by aspirations gone?

See how the sweet sun on our cliff-tops shines;
Sweeter than suns that thread meandering vines;
  There is not any greater God or purer
Than the strong God within the soul of each:
  Nor God-inspired majestic record surer
Than the long centuries of English speech.

Lo! in the gathered voice of English song
Is God, than Gods of Jewish speech more strong,
  Than all the Hellenic oracles supremer,
Than Christ's own crown and spirit more divine:
  England rise up! thou slow of heart, thou
    dreamer!
Lo! here is God, and not in Palestine!

M

Lo! here to-day the high God stands before
Thy face O England and his feet thy floor
  Impress, and he within thy blue waves singeth
And on the green slopes of thy thousand hills:
    Be blind no more,—see all the bloom he
      bringeth,
Mark how his endless hand thy summer fills.

Traitor thou art: yea traitor to thy Lord,
And murderer of thy God with foolish sword:
  He stands before thee, and thou dost not know
    him
But wanderest in the Palestinian vales;
    Yea, blind, inane and vain, thou dost forego him
And Eastward spreadest soulless fatuous sails.

Traitor thou art, O England! rise up now
And gaze towards thine own sky with fearless
    brow:
  Hear thou within the music of thy waters
The many-voiced fair psalm of God thy king;
    Mark in the flower-sweet white forms of thy
      daughters
The fairest blossoms that the ages bring.

Christ's voice was sweet, but sweeter is thine own
O England, and a loftier seat thy throne
  Than his throne; O Lord Christ shalt thou for
    ever
Rule with thine alien sceptre young great lands?
    Shall these rise up full-grown, defiant, never?
Is there no foot against thy foot that stands?

Yea, I stand forth to-day in England's name
And through my song upon my fellows shame
　　I cry in that they spread not fearless pinions,
And haply so transcend thee in the air,
　　Reaching auguster spirit-high dominions,
Finding a Father's bosom yet more fair !

A tenderer Mother-God in star-strewn night,
A kinglier Father-God within the bright
　　Abode of day ; king Christ, thou art usurper
Of English hearts ! thy crown shall pass away,
　　Thy chant be but as tongue of linnet-chirper
.　To future nightingales' full-voicèd lay.

The age advances : lo ! the white waves break
With thunder upon thunder, and they take
　　The trembling shore by inches ; art thou stable
When all life's sands and rocks are insecure ?
　　Thine empire rotten, and thy creed a fable,
Shalt thou, the unsuccessful prince, endure ?

Successful art thou, and triumphant, king !
Victorious and snow-white thine outspread wing !
　　But not victorious as the priests who crown
　　　　thee,
Victorious only through the simple soul :
　　In waves of blood these friends of thine would
　　　　drown thee,
And tides of blood above thy followers roll.

The soul of man is thine; and thine own town :
Jerusalem thou hast for seal and crown,   .
   But not the towers of ours the Western
      nations,
Yea, not the roses of our English fields !
   Offerings of Easterns, sacrifice, oblations,
But not the corn the white chalk-cliff-top yields.

Thou hast for handmaids English maidens frail
Who turned at thy presumptuous coming pale,
   Forsook their English lover-souls and gave thee
What feeble power of passion-joy they knew :
   Thou hast not, nor shouldst have from hell to
      save thee,
One great soul of one English woman true.

Rest thou content with glances dark and hold
Thine hand from meddling with bright locks of
      gold :
   Test not the Northern heart or Northern
      weather
But dwell thou in thy balmy Palestine,
   Thine olive-skinned lithe loves and thou to-
      gether,
Thou hast no rule where English grey eyes shine.

TO BEATRICE.

I.

The swift years follow
Each other, and hollow
As we grow older their voices sound;
    Now dim behind us,
    A sun to blind us
Once, yea sun-sweet o'er the charmed bright
    ground,
    Shines love, low-gleaming,
    Like red sun dreaming
Behind dark forest or green far mound.

II.

Still, still there quiver
The ripples of river,
The snow-white sheets of the sea-born foam;
    The meadow-sweet lifted
    By June-breeze, drifted
In soft bloom-powder, doth flutter and roam
    The wood-glades deep
    Where our dreams sleep,
Sleep, and abide in their fair old home.

III.

There roses many,
For us not any,
Blossom ; new lovers their bloom shall seek ;
New face of maiden
With new love laden
Shall flame in the forest, and new lips speak
The same soft message
Of sweet calm presage;
New tides, white-footed, charge up the creek.

IV.*

Apollo and love
Yet hover above
The chaste green woodland ; singers are there;
Birds in the larches,
And under the arches
Of grim grey tall trees, echo their fair
And yearly delight,
And gold through the night
Falls gently the flood of the wood-nymphs' hair..

V.

These yet abide,
Through the years deride
Our love, our pleasure, our hopes of things
That pass swift-sweeping,
Their dim eyes weeping,
Now by us and fly us on dank dark wings ;
The old same splendour
Of meadow-sweet tender
In one white flush to the moist dale clings.

VI.

Thou art not there
O woman, O fair
Long-lost loved spirit of early days ;
Then oh where art thou,
And where thy heart, thou
Who wanderest from me in flowerless ways
Where is no singing,
Yea, no voice ringing
For ever as ever with changeless praise.

VII.

The years escape us,
The long months drape us
In wearisome mantle of deepening gloom ;
Oh dost thou, lady,
Dream of the shady
Dell where we met when the rose was in bloom
And the white small lily
Starlike the hilly
Dear northland gladdened, with love's perfume ?

VIII.

Green were the alleys
Of woods, the valleys
Were bright with summer, the soft still streams
Dappled the meadows
With silver; the shadows
Of evening made more tender the dreams
The stars and the moon
Took charge of soon
Splendescent, and crowned with viewless gleams.

IX.

But not by one light
Shone love,—the sunlight
Flamed through the glittering afternoon
On lovers in corn-fields
Where laughter is born, fields
Sweet as the meads of the sky the moon
Divides demurely
With white foot, purely
Rousing in all hearts love's sure tune.

X.

Wonderful laughter
Of thine years after
Rang sweet within me, O girlish queen!
Wonderful gladness
That smote the sadness
Of all the black strange years between
Came on the heels of it,
Chimed in the peals of it,
As though no night of our sorrow had been.

XI.

Still by me I hear it,
Tender and clear it
Rings out, gentle and pure as of old;
Again I am near thee
And watch thee and hear thee,
Yea, in my hand thine hand I hold,
And the laughter deathless
Trembling and breathless
Keeps me, superb from the mouth of gold.

XII.

O golden girl-mouth,
　　Though time's waves swirl, mouth,
About thee, they hinder no throb of song;
　　They choke thy laughter
　　Never for after
Their passing sweet as before and as strong
　　The dear laugh ringeth,
　　To my soul clingeth,
Drowneth the years' wails weary and long.

XIII.

Ten years between us
　　Serve but to screen us
The better from others, the closer to draw
　　Our hearts together,
　　As in wild weather
Souls cling more closely and ice-hearts thaw,
　　When some tossed vessel
　　Rises to wrestle
With thundering waves that follow and awe.

XIV.

So as we rise
　　To battle with skies
Of later lifetime and waves whose sound
　　Struggles to 'whelm
　　Our tired-out helm,
And shoals where many a keel doth ground,
　　The old green bowers
　　Beckon, and hours
Come back, forgotten, but now new-found.

XV.

How hath death revelled
'Mid locks dishevelled
Since at our feet the stream lisped low!
How many have left us,
Dark arrows have cleft us,
Arrows sped from the death-god's bow :
And though Apollo
The death-god follow,
Some sad seeds hath he of song to sow.

XVI.

The golden harp-string
Is sometimes sharp string
And hath its message of sorrow and grief;
Sometimes autumnal
The song-god's hymnal
Seems, and saddened the song-god's leaf
With hues as of death,
And the song-god's breath
Like a wounded bird's breath, bitter and brief.

XVII.

Therefore I dying
Or living, relying
On Fate, on woman, on man, or on him
Who some souls urges
With vehement surges
Of song, that they cease not till eyes grow dim,
Across time's torrent,
Ten years' red current,
Gaze—as across a sea-strait grim.

XVIII.

My whole soul yearns to thee,
Weeps, and turns to thee,
Lady, so far in the years behind:
Thy breath comes sadly,
Yet not ungladly,
Just as the waft of a rose on the wind,
And thy voice clearly
Whispereth nearly;
My spirit by the old waves I find.

XIX.

Thou art not altered,
Nor have I faltered
In my clear mission of endless song:
If death should seize us,
His cold touch freeze us,
Long ere a decade as sad, as long,
Pass once more by us,
He may not deny us
The past, its beauty, its love-voice strong.

XX.

Death cannot foil us
Wholly, despoil us
Of one sweet love-throb that e'er hath leapt
Through the bosom that bounded
As some foot sounded,
Dear to us, clear to us,—near to us stept;
The old woods yet the same for us
With song-flowers flame for us,
Though ten years' summers have dawned and have
slept.

Feb. 13, 1880.

TO THE UNCHANGED GOD.

I.

Thou changest never
Though men change ever,
Yea, veer as waves of the shifting tides ;
Our seasons pass,
We wither as grass
That lies burnt brown on the mountain's sides ;
But thou remainest
And death disdainest,
Thy firm foot over the centuries strides.

II.

When Rome was young
Thy lips in it sung,
The Grecian hill-sides caught from thee
Their rose-red light
Of joy ; in the night
Of unknown eras thou wast, and the sea
Has known thee, O Lord,
And its music has poured
Forth for thee since ever it came to be.

III.

When we look back
And a flower in the track
Behold and cling to, where passion hath been
In the sweet dim past for us,
A blossom to last for us,
A white soft-centred memory, a queen,
We are but a part
Of thy changeless heart,
Thine endless spirit, kingly, serene.

IV.

Thou art in the bowers
Of memory, the flowers
The long years gather and treasure and keep :
In first love's tender
And infinite splendour,
O infinite God, thine eyes too weep :
And thou dost delight
In the calm of the night
When lovers upon thy soft breast sleep.

V.

Not one white rose
Without thee blows,
Thou art in the meadows that smile in the morn ;
The long grey hills
Thy presence fills,
And the roar of the breakers is thy strong scorn ;
And summer divine
Is surely thine,
And all its scents at thy word are born.

VI.

We are but a dream,
We live not, we seem
To live, but our living is over and past
In the hours of a day;
Yet thou dost stay,
Thy beauty fades not, thy breath doth last
Fragrant as long
As the roses throng
The green earth, down to it pink leaves cast.

VII.

Me singing to-day
The self same lay
That David sang or Apollo or bard
Of unknown city,
Time shall not pity;
No passion may death's pale foot retard;
The singers of old .
Are silent and cold,
The fire of time their harps hath charred.

VIII.

Ruth in the corn
As a flower was born
For a season: she passed to the death-god's hold;
The red corn-poppies
Her fading copies,
She faded as faded the corn-ears gold
'Mid which she gleaned
When the strong man leaned
Eager to watch her, ardent of old.

IX.

Helen is gone,
The lips are wan
That once to fetter had but to speak;
The strange great queen
In the shades is seen—
The moons of the shades lie soft on the cheek
Which Antony kissed;
Now the winds and the mist
Of Lethe alone the white shape seek.

X.

How many were fair
In the dense mid-air
Of the clustered ages that gave the west
Its glory and crown;
Their loves, their renown,
Their very names, 'mid the dead flowers rest;
Iseult is dead
And the crowned gold head
Of Guinevere; grasses cling to her breast.

XI.

And swift-soul Mary
Who came with fairy
Dreams in her clear gaze, flowers in her hand
To charm all mortals,
Hath passed the portals
That open upon the songless land;
The black gates clang,
And the voice that rang
Is hushed, and the white feet far from us stand.

XII.

So surely a season
Of sudden dark treason
Of death is coming to each and all;
But changeless thou
God laughest, as now
Before thy winter the frail flowers fall;
As cold snows settle
On thin rose-petal,
And ivy straggles o'er tower and hall.

XIII.

To-day we sing to you,
Our swift songs cling to you,
O world of blossoms we soon shall leave;
But what of to-morrow?
Will it bring sorrow?
Will some for our passing sigh once and grieve?
A singer to-day
Like a bird on a spray
Clings to the world's branch; will it receive?

XIV.

Will it receive him,
Sadden or leave him,—
He for a day sings, only a day;
Others shall follow,
Never Apollo
Hath not a song-word potent to say;
But what world takes them,
As this forsakes them,
The singers whom this world's gods betray?

XV.

We pass through the flowers,
World, of your bowers,
And some we gather and some disdain;
We pluck in your valleys
The flower-wreath that tallies
Best with the song-flowers born in our strain;
And then we fold
Our plumelets of gold,
Or of grey, and quit you : our songs remain.

XVI.

But oh whither we
Depart, to what sea
With strange dark waves, what garden, what bower,
Who knows or can say?
What summer-sweet day
Awaits us, or sorrowful ice-filled shower?
What guerdon to win?
What joys gathered in?
What rose of new passion, unspeakable flower?

XVII.

Are there women as white
In the bowers of the night
Of death as in rose-hung bowers of the day?
Are there faces as fair
In that desolate air

Where the wings of the hours hang sodden and
   grey ?
        Are there mouths that can kiss ?
        Is there infinite bliss
Of love, or doth all love vanish away ?

XVIII.

      No soul can reply :
      From that mystical sky
Come but faint murmurs, no clear voice rings
      Downward in answer,
      And but a romancer
Seems each one who message inadequate brings
      From that strange far land,
      Weirder than star-land,
Whence throbs all music on monstrous wings.

XIX.

      For music is death,
      And God, and the breath
Of new-born flowers who change may defy ;
      The lips of the Lord
      Through its cadences poured
In it thunder and laugh and reward and reply ;
      In it seas of the speech
      Of God on the beach
Of time plunge downward from fathomless skv.

XX.

      But all else changes
      As time's foot ranges
Pitiless, ceaseless, over our plains ;

His barren relentless
Blossomless scentless
Finger the date of our death retains;
And lo! as we sing
A sudden soft wing,
Death's, darkens the chamber and hushed are our
strains.

Printed by REMINGTON & Co., 133, New Bond Street, W.

Trieste

Trieste Publishing has a massive catalogue of classic book titles. Our aim is to provide readers with the highest quality reproductions of fiction and non-fiction literature that has stood the test of time. The many thousands of books in our collection have been sourced from libraries and private collections around the world.

The titles that Trieste Publishing has chosen to be part of the collection have been scanned to simulate the original. Our readers see the books the same way that their first readers did decades or a hundred or more years ago. Books from that period are often spoiled by imperfections that did not exist in the original. Imperfections could be in the form of blurred text, photographs, or missing pages. It is highly unlikely that this would occur with one of our books. Our extensive quality control ensures that the readers of Trieste Publishing's books will be delighted with their purchase. Our staff has thoroughly reviewed every page of all the books in the collection, repairing, or if necessary, rejecting titles that are not of the highest quality. This process ensures that the reader of one of Trieste Publishing's titles receives a volume that faithfully reproduces the original, and to the maximum degree possible, gives them the experience of owning the original work.

We pride ourselves on not only creating a pathway to an extensive reservoir of books of the finest quality, but also providing value to every one of our readers. Generally, Trieste books are purchased singly - on demand, however they may also be purchased in bulk. Readers interested in bulk purchases are invited to contact us directly to enquire about our tailored bulk rates. Email: customerservice@triestepublishing.com

You May Also Like

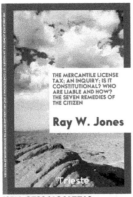

The Mercantile License Tax; An Inquiry; Is It Constitutional? Who Are Liable and How? The Seven Remedies of the Citizen

Ray W. Jones

ISBN: 9780649647743
Paperback: 126 pages
Dimensions: 6.14 x 0.27 x 9.21 inches
Language: eng

Our Glorified. Poems and Passages of Consolation Especially for Those Bereaved by the Loss of Children

Elizabeth Howard Foxcroft

ISBN: 9780649665013
Paperback: 149 pages
Dimensions: 5.83 x 0.32 x 8.27 inches
Language: eng

You May Also Like

The University of Chicago, Department of Political Economy; The Economic History of the Hawaiian Islands. A Dissertation

U. S. Parker

ISBN: 9780649568093
Paperback: 133 pages
Dimensions: 6.14 x 0.29 x 9.21 inches
Language: eng

Hymns on the Psalms

Anonymous

ISBN: 9780649610211
Paperback: 156 pages
Dimensions: 6.14 x 0.33 x 9.21 inches
Language: eng

You May Also Like

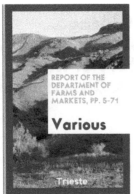

ISBN: 9780649333158
Paperback: 84 pages
Dimensions: 6.14 x 0.17 x 9.21 inches
Language: eng

Report of the Department of Farms and Markets, pp. 5-71

Various

ISBN: 9780649324132
Paperback: 78 pages
Dimensions: 6.14 x 0.16 x 9.21 inches
Language: eng

Catalogue of the Episcopal Theological School in Cambridge Massachusetts, 1891-1892

Various

www.triestepublishing.com

You May Also Like

Three Hundred Tested Recipes

Various

ISBN: 9780649352142
Paperback: 88 pages
Dimensions: 6.14 x 0.18 x 9.21 inches
Language: eng

A Basket of Fragments

Anonymous

ISBN: 9780649419418
Paperback: 108 pages
Dimensions: 6.14 x 0.22 x 9.21 inches
Language: eng

Find more of our titles on our website. We have a selection of thousands of titles that will interest you. Please visit

www.triestepublishing.com

Printed in Australia
AUHW011000310321
343452AU00007B/13

9 780649 502469